Fodor's
25Best

LISBON

How to Use
This Book

 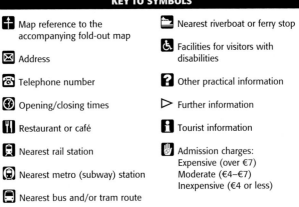
This guide is divided into four sections
• Essential Lisbon: An introduction to the city and tips on making the most of your stay.
• Lisbon by Area: We've broken the city into six areas, and recommended the best sights, shops, entertainment venues, nightlife and restaurants in each one. Suggested walks help you to explore on foot.
• Where to Stay: The best hotels, whether you're looking for luxury, budget or something in between.
• Need to Know: The info you need to make your trip run smoothly, including getting about by public transport, weather tips, emergency phone numbers and useful websites.

Navigation In the Lisbon by Area chapter, we've given each area its own color, which is also used on the locator maps throughout the book and the map on the inside front cover.

Maps The fold-out map with this book is a comprehensive street plan of Lisbon. The grid on this fold-out map is the same as the grid on the locator maps within the book. We've given grid references within the book for each sight and listing.

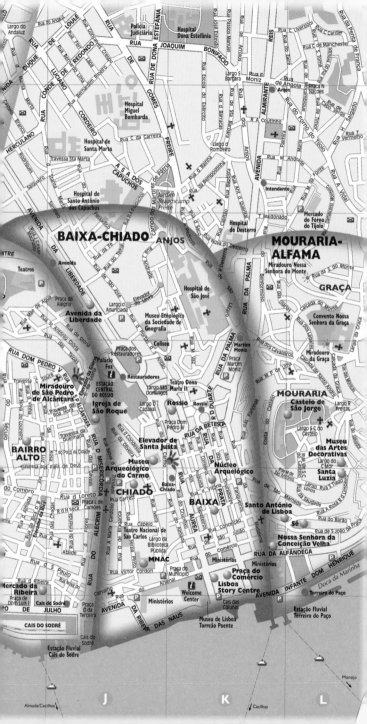

Contents

Introducing Lisbon

Lisbon is a perfect mix of old and new, a glorious remnant of a once-powerful maritime empire mixed with a dynamic, forward-looking city of considerable cultural and social élan. The quietly ageing capital has evolved into a modern city.

While shaking off the worst of the past, the city has retained much of the quirky and unpretentious charm that makes it such a pleasure to visit. Modern office buildings and shopping malls may sprout across the city, muscling in on an atmospheric medley of Moorish and medieval quarters, but in their shadow you will still find streets full of rattling old trams, crumbling mansions, walls of beautiful tiles, mosaic pavements, lovely churches, festive markets and any number of glorious old bars and cafés, where the traditional conversational certainties of football, family and religion still hold sway.

The social and cultural changes wrought by greater prosperity have made their mark in Lisbon. The city's new cultural swagger was first made manifest on a grand scale in 1994, when Lisbon was named European City of Culture, and continues today in dazzling cultural complexes such as the Centro Cultural de Belém (▷ 94). It's also apparent in the new funky shops and smart galleries of contemporary art in the Bairro Alto and elsewhere, and in the city's artists and brash young fashion designers, who confidently show their work in London, Paris and New York.

Lisbon's transformation has been dramatic and quick, and in the wrench that pulled it virtually from the 19th to the 21st century in less than a generation, some people—and places—were inevitably left behind. The global recession that hit in 2008 brought the rapid progress to a halt, and both city and country are still recovering. Yet, despite the turbulence of recent years, this is a city where the old charm will never entirely disappear.

FACTS AND FIGURES

● Lisbon is Europe's most westerly city.
● The population of Lisbon is about 545,000.
● The population of Greater Lisbon and the Tagus valley combined is around 3,340,000—about a third of Portugal's total population.
● The Lisbon area produces 45 percent of Portugal's GDP.

TRAMS

A great way to see contemporary Lisbon is on one of the city's oldest means of public transport. Trams have been rattling around Lisbon's streets since 1901. Today they run on 72km (45 miles) of track. Take the 28 tram for a memorable sightseeing tour, or the 15 from Praça da Figueira to Belém for a look at one of the city's modern super-trams.

TILES

Tiles, or *azulejos*, are found almost everywhere in Lisbon. "*Azulejos*" comes from the Arab word *al azulaycha*, which means "polished little stone". The Moors introduced the art of tile-making to the Iberian peninsula in the eighth century. Tiles are still used in many contemporary buildings, notably the Cais do Sodré and other metro stations.

MODERN CITY

Lisbon's stunning contemporary architecture includes the Armazéns do Chiado (▷ 32) and Peter Chermayeff's Oceanário, the Ponte Vasco da Gama and Álvaro Siza Vieira's extraordinary curved concrete roof for the Pavilhão de Portugal. These architectural marvels are located at the Parque das Nações (▷ 102–103), designed for the 1998 World Expo.

A Short Stay in Lisbon

DAY 1

Morning Start your day in the medieval district of Lisbon, the **Alfama** (▷ 42–43). Walk or take tram 12 or 28 up to the **Sé** (▷ 48–49), Lisbon's imposing cathedral. Go up to the **Miradoura de Santa Luzia**—you can take a tram—for splendid views over the harbor.

Mid-morning Stop for a coffee at the **Café Cerca Moura** (▷ 54), close by the mirador. Continue up to visit the **Museu das Artes Decorativas** (▷ 47), housed in a beautiful 17th-century palace. Cut up the steep streets behind the museum to reach the **Castelo de São Jorge** (▷ 44).

Lunch You can take lunch in the castle grounds or alternatively wander down the narrow streets of the Alfama to eat later. Walk or take a tram down to **Praça do Comércio** (▷ 26), where you can have a snack in the popular **Café Martinho da Arcada** (▷ 36–37) or stroll along to **Ibo** (▷ 38) at Cais do Sodré.

Afternoon From the square take the fast tram 15 to visit the Belém district. Get off at the stop after the monastery, so you can start your visit at a gem of a building, the **Torre de Belém** (▷ 92–93). You can then board the open-air mini-train, which takes you to all the scattered sights of Belém, or continue by foot. Highlights include the monument **Padrão dos Descobrimentos** (▷ 91), the **Museu Coleção Berardo** (▷ 88–89) and **Centro Cultural de Belém** (▷ 94), the **Mosteiro dos Jerónimos** (▷ 86–87) and the **Museu Nacional dos Coches** (▷ 90).

Dinner Try the restaurant **Cais de Belém** (▷ 96), overlooking the park.

Evening Head back to town or take tram 15 or the train to the water-front hot spot Alcântara, with its restaurants, bars and clubs.

DAY 2

Morning Start in **Praça do Comércio** (▷ 26) and walk through the arch to Rua Augusta to wander the grid of streets and check out the shopping. Head for Rua Áurea and let the **Elevador de Santa Justa** (▷ 30) whisk you up into Chiado, giving you great views. Walk up Rua do Carmo, with lots more shopping opportunities.

Mid-morning Continue on to Rua Garrett, pausing at Lisbon's most famous coffeehouse, **Café a Brasileira** (▷ 36). The streets to the north have some of the best shops in the city or you could visit the **Museu Arqueológico** (▷ 25) in Largo do Carmo. Walk downhill, or take the elevator, and make your way to **Rossio** (▷ 27), Lisbon's central square.

Lunch Head to Rua das Portas de Santo Antão, just north of the square, for a choice of restaurants. Try **Casa do Alentejo** (▷ 37) for traditional fare or, for fish, the more expensive **Gambrinus** (▷ 38).

Afternoon Take the green line metro from Rossio and change at Alameda for the red line to Oriente. This brings you to the **Parque das Nações** (▷ 102–103), the site of Expo 98, with its excellent science museum and aquarium—great for kids. There is a lot to do and see here and you might want to stay on into the evening.

Dinner Have a meal at the Parque or head back to the **Bairro Alto** (▷ 58) to Rua do Diario de Noticias/Rua Atalaia area (Baixa-Chiado metro), with international restaurants such as the Argentinian **Último Tango** (▷ 72).

Evening This district is famous for its traditional fado music—try **Arcadas do Faia** or **Adega do Machado** (▷ 68). This is also the place to go for bars, many of which feature live music and stay open very late.

►►►

Alfama ▷ 42–43 The old part of the city, with narrow streets and evocative cafés, set beneath the castle.

Bairro Alto ▷ 58 Once the haunt of artists, this district is a popular nightspot with its bars and restaurants.

Baixa ▷ 24 A grid of 18th-century streets running down from Rossio to the Praça do Comércio.

Torre de Belém ▷ 92–93 The attractive UNESCO Heritage Site was built to protect Lisbon's harbor.

Shopping in Chiado ▷ 28–29 A lovely area with some of the most elegant shops and boutiques in Lisbon.

Sé ▷ 48–49 Imposing cathedral, rebuilt after the 1755 earthquake, but retaining some original features.

Rossio ▷ 27 Bustling central meeting place, perfect for people-watching, that has witnessed some turbulent times in the past.

Praça do Comércio ▷ 26 Majestic square by the waterfront, with a triumphal arch leading from the sea into the city.

Parque das Nações ▷ 102–103 Impressive and thriving cultural waterside development originally built for Expo 98.

Palácio dos Marqueses de Fronteira ▷ 78–79 Lovely palace, just a metro ride away in the suburbs.

Padrão dos Descobrimentos ▷ 91 The monument reaches out toward the sea.

Museu Nacional dos Coches ▷ 90 Splendid coaches and carriages built for royalty and nobility.

These pages are a quick guide to the Top 25, which are described in more detail later. Here they are listed alphabetically, and the tinted background shows which area they are in.

Basílica da Estrela ▷ 59
Dominating the surrounding area, this impressive church affords great views.

Castelo de São Jorge ▷ 44 You can't avoid seeing this fine castle from all over the city.

Centro de Arte Moderna ▷ 80 Get acquainted with Portuguese artists at this stylish gallery.

Fado in Alfama ▷ 45
This heart-wrenching musical form is at its best when it's a spontaneous outburst.

Feira da Ladra ▷ 46
Bustling flea market centered in the Campo de Santa Clara.

Igreja de São Roque ▷ 60–61 Elaborately decorated church with a wonderful collection of tiles.

Mosteiro dos Jerónimos ▷ 86–87 Superb 16th-century monastery in Belém.

Museu Arqueológico do Carmo ▷ 25 Eccentric, but interesting collection.

Museu das Artes Decorativas ▷ 47 Beautiful 17th-century palace displaying a wonderful collection of objects.

Museu Calouste Gulbenkian ▷ 76–77 Portugal's single greatest museum.

Museu Nacional do Azulejo ▷ 100–101 Great museum dedicated to the celebrated *azulejo*, or tile.

Museu Nacional de Arte Antiga ▷ 62–63 A fine collection of art and decorative objects.

Museu Coleção Berardo ▷ 88–89 Portugal's finest contemporary art collection has a home at last.

Map labels:

Parque das Nações
CAMPO PEQUENO
OLAIAS
Praça de Touros
REGO
Museu Calouste Gulbenkian
Parque de Palhavã
Centro de Arte Moderna
ARCO CEGO
ALTO DO PINA
SALDANHA
Parque Eduardo VII
ESTEFÂNIA
Cemitério do Alto de São João
PENHA DE FRANÇA
SÃO SEBASTIÃO
Museu Nacional do Azulejo
DREIRAS
Jardim Braamcamp Freire
BAIRRO ALTO / THE WEST
Jardim Botânico
ANJOS
BAIXA-CHIADO
20–38
MOURARIA-ALFAMA
39–54
RATO
GRAÇA
MOURARIA
Feira da Ladra
RELA
Igreja de São Roque
Rossio
Castelo de São Jorge
Fado
BAIRRO ALTO
Museu Arqueológico do Carmo
ALFAMA
Museu das Artes Decorativas
DRAGOA
CHIADO
BAIXA
Sé
Praça do Comércio

9

Shopping

Lisbon is not a shopper's haven compared with London, Paris or New York, but the city does score high for its range of traditional and specialist shops, and in its prices, which, for certain goods, notably shoes and leatherware, are some of the lowest in Western Europe. The city's gentle pace makes it an ideal place for relaxed browsing, but for a more dynamic experience visit one of the city's popular shopping malls.

Traditional Roots

The main shopping areas are easily defined. The key area has always been the Baixa, whose central grid of streets—unlike those of many modern cities—still retains a wonderful array of traditional and designer stores. Behind the tiny shopfronts, many with lovely art deco facades, you'll find everything from Louis Vuitton and La Perla to dusty cobblers and pungent old grocers' stores piled with cheeses, vintage port and other Portuguese staples. Many of the specialist shops here have been run continuously by the same family of craftspeople for centuries.

Cutting-Edge Style

The steep narrow streets of the Bairro Alto district contain an altogether more cutting-edge collection of shops, including many small designer fashion outlets, modern furniture showrooms and eccentric stores that reflect the area's chic, bohemian feel. Much the same can

You can pick up a souvenir of Lisbon at the excellent range of individual shops

EAT AND SHOP CARD

Lisbon's Turismo de Lisboa produces various discount cards and other passes (▷ 118), including the Lisboa Eat and Shop Card. Costing €6, and valid for 72 hours, this give a discount of 10 percent at over 30 participating restaurants and between 5–10 percent at more than a hundred shops. It is available at all tourist information outlets. For details, see visitlisboa.com. If you're paying cash in some of the more traditional and artisan stores, it's worth asking for a discount.

be said of the adjacent Chiado, though here the prices are higher and the stores more exclusive. Most big names appear on Avenida da Liberdade, with price tags rising the farther north you go.

Shopping Malls
Most of the shopping malls are more outlying, though this does nothing to deter *Lisboetas*, who seem to have taken modern malls to their hearts—the biggest and best are Amoreiras, Colombo and Centro Comercial Vasco da Gama (▷ 102–103). At the other extreme, Lisbon has plenty of down-to-earth street markets, many worth visiting as much for their local atmosphere as for their bargains (▷ below).

Value for Money
Among Lisbon's best buys, shoes and leatherware are often inexpensive—though styles and sizes may be limited—as are some of the country's traditional foods and wines. You'll often find vintage port, along with other foodstuffs, at good prices in the supermarkets. Tiles (*azulejos*) and ceramics are also good buys and make excellent souvenirs to take home, as do wooden crafts, linens and other textiles. Antiques are never inexpensive, but you'll find a good selection in and around the Bairro Alto, especially in the shops on Rua de São Bento and Rua Dom Pedro V.

MARKETS

One of Lisbon's most lively shopping experiences is the Feira da Ladra (🕐 Tue and Sat 7am–1pm), a flea market at Campo de Santa Clara in the Alfama district (▷ 46). Many stalls sell little more than junk, but there are also stalls with decent antiques, clothes, CDs, handicrafts and more. The best of the food and general markets is the Mercado Ribeira on Avenida 24 de Julho (▷ 65), a short walk from Cais do Sodré. Various theme markets take place on Sunday at the Parque das Nações (▷ 102–103), above the metro station, ranging from stamps and coins to handicrafts, antiques and decorative arts.

Shopping by Theme

Whether you're looking for a department store, a quirky boutique, or something in between, you'll find it all in Lisbon. On this page shops are listed by theme. For a more detailed write-up, see the individual listings in Lisbon by Area.

Lisbon by Night

Not so long ago, nightlife in Lisbon consisted of little more than a handful of old bars, restaurants and the occasional live entertainment in the shape of fado (▷ 45, 53). But as the rest of the city has changed, so has its nightlife, and today Lisbon has a huge selection of cutting-edge bars and state-of-the-art venues, as well as one of Europe's most dynamic clubbing scenes.

Where to Party

Much of the action takes place in the Bairro Alto, whose many sleek bars, clubs and lounges heave with up to 50,000 people on the busiest evenings of the week. As the night wears on, many of these revelers drift west to the clubs on Avenida 24 de Julho, or to the Alcântara, a rejuvenated dock area whose waterfront—especially the Doca de Santo Amaro—has been almost entirely given over to late-opening, warehouse-style bars and clubs. Clubbers have also moved east, to the even newer nightlife districts of the Parque das Nações (▷ 102) and Santa Apolónia waterfront.

A Little More Sedate

City nightlife need not be a frantic round of clubs. There are occasional operas and other classical music concerts, many staged outdoors when the weather allows. And on a summer evening, of course, nightlife need consist of no more than a relaxing meal under the stars, a quiet drink in an atmospheric bar or a balmy evening stroll through some of the old city's more sedate streets.

...mospheric Lisbon by ...ht—from traditional ...o haunts to the most ...dern of venues

NIGHTLIFE ETIQUETTE

Lisbon's bar and club scene does not really get going until midnight. Many clubs have an admission charge—anything up to €30—which might include one or two drinks (admission may be free on quieter weekdays). On entry, there may also be a *consumo mínimo*, or minimum consumption charge. Bouncers can refuse admission if the club is full, or if you are underdressed.

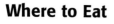

Where to Eat

Portugal has suffered a bad press where cuisine is concerned, with many a menu unchanged for more than 30 years. However, with a more cosmopolitan approach to life, Lisbon is seeing a change in cooking, albeit with the traditional elements still to be found.

Portuguese Roots

There is a tradition of simple, wholesome food in the country and this is retained in many recipes today. Seafood and fresh fish are as popular as ever, but with all that fresh fish available, it is perhaps difficult to understand the Portuguese love of the ubiquitous *bacalhau* (dried salt cod). It was first introduced way back when the Portuguese caught the cod off the shores of Newfoundland, bringing it home to be salted, dried and preserved. There is said to be a different recipe for *bacalhau* for each day of the year, but many find it an acquired taste. You will come across many traditional dishes in Lisbon, but they are increasingly produced in a more innovative way.

Eating Times

Start the day as the *Lisboetas* do, with a pastry and strong coffee, standing up at the bar in true European style. Lunch is a robust affair, usually taken between 12.30 and 2pm. This should keep you going until dinner, which is often not taken until 8pm (or later at the weekend), but you will find tourists packing the restaurants as early as 7pm.

SARDINES

This humble fish is close to the hearts of the people of Portugal and in Lisbon the beginning of summer is heralded by the opening of the sardine season. With the onset of the warmer nights and the celebration of the patron saint of Lisbon, St. Antony, on 13 June, grilled sardines become a focal point. Eaten with boiled potatoes and salad, and often served on a piece of bread, they are washed down with white *vinho verde*, red wine or beer.

Eat out under the blue sky, on a shaded terrace or in a garden, or indoors in traditional surroundings

Where to Eat by Cuisine

There are plenty of places to eat to suit all tastes and budgets in Lisbon. On this page they are listed by cuisine. For a more detailed description of each restaurant, see Lisbon by Area.

Cafés/Pastelarias

Antiga Casa dos Pastéis de Belém (▷ 96)
Café a Brasileira (▷ 36)
Café Cerca Moura (▷ 54)
Café Martinho da Arcada (▷ 36)
Café Nicola (▷ 37)
Casa Chineza (▷ 37)
Confeitaria Nacional (▷ 37)
Pastelaria Bénard (▷ 38)
Pastelaria-Padaria São Roque (▷ 71)
Pastelaria Suiça (▷ 38)

Fine Dining

Casa da Comida (▷ 70)
Confraria at York House (▷ 71)
Tavares (▷ 38)

International

Ali-à-Papa (▷ 70)
Casanova (▷ 54)
Comida de Santo (▷ 70)
Picanha (▷ 72)
Último Tango (▷ 72)

Light Meals/Snacks

Alfaia (▷ 70)
Bonjardim (▷ 36)
Café no Chiado (▷ 37)
Casa Faz Frio (▷ 70)
Enoteca Chafariz do Vinho (▷ 71)
Portugália (▷ 72)

Most Fashionable

Bica do Sapato (▷ 54)
Espaço Lisboa (▷ 71)
L'Entrecote (▷ 38)
Solar dos Nunes (▷ 72)
XL (▷ 72)

Seafood

Cervejaria Pinóquio (▷ 37)
Fidalgo (▷ 71)
Gambrinus (▷ 38)
Ibo (Cais da Ribeira) (▷ 38)
Mercado do Peixe (▷ 96)
Ribadouro (▷ 72)
Solmar (▷ 38)

Traditional

1° de Maio (▷ 70)
Bota Alta (▷ 70)
Cais de Belém (▷ 96)
Casa do Alentejo (▷ 37)
Cervejaria Trindade (▷ 37)
Lautasco (▷ 54)
Malmequer Bemmequer (▷ 54)
O Carvoeiro (▷ 96)
O Caseiro (▷ 96)
Pap'açorda (▷ 71)
Portugalia (▷ 96)
Primavera (▷ 72)
Via Graça (▷ 54)

Top Tips For...

These great suggestions will help you tailor your ideal visit to Lisbon, no matter how you choose to spend your time. Each sight or listing has a fuller write-up elsewhere in the book.

PORTUGUESE CUISINE

For food from the Alentejo region try **Casa do Alentejo** (▷ 37).
Sample *bacalhau* (salt cod) at Casa Faz Frio (▷ 70), renowned for this traditional dish.
Inexpensive but tasty traditional fare can be found at **Malmequer Bemmequer** (▷ 54).
There are typical specialties to sample at **Portugalia** (▷ 96), a good option when exploring Belém.

HISTORIC CAFÉS

The most famous of all is the **Café a Brasileira** (▷ 36) in the Bairro Alto.
Café Nicola (▷ 37) has been serving customers since 1777.
One of Lisbon's finest cafés is **Pastelaria Bénard** (▷ 38)—try the desserts.
Watch the world go by from an outside table at **Café Martinho da Arcada** (▷ 36), founded in the 18th century.

A PALATIAL STAY

Palácio de Belmonte (▷ 112) is one of the world's finest small hotels.
Stay at a historic hotel like **Pestana Palace** (▷ 112), set in fabulous grounds.
A 19th-century palace with a beautiful garden is home to the **Lapa Palace** (▷ 112), Lisbon's classiest, and most expensive, 5-star hotel.

LISBON ON A BUDGET

Big portions are the order of the day at low-price **Bota Alta** restaurant (▷ 70).
Visit the **Museu Calouste Gulbenkian**, Lisbon's greatest museum, on a Sunday—it's free (▷ 76–77).

Clockwise from top left: typical fish dish; Jardim Guerra Junqueiro; port and tiles make ideal gifts; the cable

A RELAXING BREAK

Enjoy the views and the exotic birds in the gardens of the **Castelo de São Jorge** (▷ 44). An oasis of calm can be found in the **Jardim Botânico** (▷ 64).

Catch a glimpse of neighborhood life and enjoy a drink by the lake while the children play in the spacious grounds of the **Jardim Guerra Junqueiro** (▷ 64).

Parque Eduardo VI (▷ 81) is Lisbon's most iconic park, with walkways, mature trees, hothouses and superb views.

Come to the enormous **Parque Florestal de Monsanto** (▷ 81) at the weekend to enjoy acres of green space, great views and free entertainment.

BUYING SOUVENIRS

For lovely Portuguese textiles and traditional knitwear, head for **Casa de Bordados de Madeira** (▷ 32).

Portuguese handicrafts of all kinds are for sale at **Alberto Santos** (▷ 32).

You'll find wonderful handcrafted artefacts, ceramics and fabrics at **Santos Oficios** (▷ 35). For all things nostalgic go to **Casa Portuguesa** (▷ 33).

TRADITIONAL TILES

The best choice of *azulejos* (tiles) to buy is at **Fábrica de Céramica Viúva Lamego** (▷ 53). The leading producer of tiles since 1741 has been **Fábrica Sant'Anna** (▷ 34), located in the Chiado district.

RIDING HIGH

The 19th-century **Elevador de Santa Justa** (▷ 30) will whisk you up the steep hill from the Baixa district to the Bairro Alto.

For another route up to Bairro Alto take the **Elevador da Glória funicular** (▷ 58).

Take the cable car and ride high over the **Parque das Nações** (▷ 102–103) for a view of the whole park.

car at Parque das Nações; Chinese porcelain in the Gulbenkian Museum; Palácio de Belmonte; Café Nicola

GOOD PLACES TO AMUSE THE CHILDREN

Oceanário (▷ 105) is just one of the great attractions for kids in the Parque das Nações (▷ 102–103).

Budding sailors will enjoy the **Museu de Marinha** maritime museum at Belém (▷ 94). Special sky shows for children take place at the **Planetário Calouste Gulbenkian** (▷ 94). Children will enjoy the interactive exhibits and activities at the **Pavilhão do Conhecimento– Ciência Viva** at the Parque das Nações (▷ 105).

TRADITIONAL MUSIC

Get to know fado music at the popular tourist spot **Clube de Fado** (▷ 53) or **O Senhor Vinho** (▷ 69).

For fado and a meal try the reasonably priced **Parreirinha de Alfama** (▷ 53).

Music and traditional folklore can be found at the historic **Café Luso** (▷ 68).

A TRENDY NIGHT-TIME SCENE

Ultra-trendy **Lux** (▷ 53) is the place to be seen, with great views over the river from the terrace.

For the most eccentric bar in town try the **Pavilhão Chinês** (▷ 69) with its walls and ceilings crammed with thousands of weird and wonderful objects.

Hot Clube Jazz (▷ 69) is the best-known and revered jazz venue in the city.

TRIPS FARTHER OUT

Parque das Nações (▷ 102–103) will keep you entertained for a full day.

If you want beautiful scenery and fabulous palaces go to **Sintra** (▷ 106).

Climb to the top of the **Cristo Rei** (▷ 66), on the other side of the River Tejo.

For an insight into the wealth of the 18th-century monarchy and a glimpse of small town life, head for **Mafra** (▷ 106), an hour or so outside Lisbon.

Oceanário; fado and jazz houses are plentiful in Lisbon; Castelo dos Mouros, in Sintra

Lisbon by Area

An inspired example of 18th-century town-grid planning, Baixa changed the face of the city. Spreading up the hill to the west, Chiado is home to museums, theaters, historic buildings, cafés and elegant shops.

Top 25

Baixa

Art deco shopfronts in the Baixa (left); an aerial view of the district at night (right)

THE BASICS

🔼 K7–K8

✉ Streets between the Rossio and Praça do Comércio

🍴 Cafés, bars and restaurants

Ⓜ Rossio/Baixa-Chiado

🚊 All services to Rossio and Praça do Comércio

♿ Poor

HIGHLIGHTS

- Art deco shopfronts
- Mosaic pavements
- Cobbled streets

Set between the hills of the Chiado and Alfama, the distinctive Baixa district, with its arrow-straight cobbled streets, magnificent main square and idiosyncratic shopfronts, is the heart of old Lisbon.

Pombal's vision A grid of ordered streets, the Baixa district stretches from the Rossio in the north to the Praça do Comércio in the south, with the Chiado rising to the west and the Alfama to the east. It is thought this low-lying area was once on a stream, with houses built on stilts to escape flooding. Its appearance was changed beyond all recognition following the 1755 earthquake, when the Marquês de Pombal decided to rebuild the area along strictly rational lines. He decreed that all new streets should be "40 feet in width, with pavements on either side protected from wheeled traffic by stone pillars, as in London".

Tradition Pombal's dream was realized with the help of a military engineer, Eugénio dos Santos, and the result has been described as one of the finest European architectural achievements of the age. The pleasing symmetry and simplicity of the architectural design are a perfect foil to the hum and buzz of daily life. There's no denying its old-fashioned charm, nor the appeal of the mosaic-patterned pavements, tiled facades and lovely old shopfronts. The pedestrianized Rua Augusta is the area's main axis. Many minor streets bear names relating to the trades once conducted there.

Housed in the ruins of a convent (left), the museum is just off Rossio square (right)

TOP 25

Museu Arqueológico do Carmo

Housed in the ruins of a convent, the eclectic and appealing collections held in the Museu Arqueológico do Carmo encompass over a thousand years of artifacts, carvings, sculpture and art.

Location The archaeological museum is within the ruins of the Convento do Carmo, a Carmelite convent built by Nuno Álvares Pereira. He was a general and companion-in-arms to João I at the Battle of Aljubarrota in 1385, which secured Portuguese independence from Castile for 200 years. Until 1755, when the convent church was toppled by the Great Earthquake, it was the largest church in the city. Over the years its ruins were used as a graveyard and military stable. Today its soaring Gothic interior is largely open to the Lisbon sky, the nave and chancel now paved with gravel and surrounded by trees.

Eccentric The museum's exhibits are a slightly disorganized and eccentric mixture, which constitutes part of their appeal. They include two tombs, one belonging to Ferdinand I, King of Portugal from 1367 to 1382, the other to Gonçalo de Souza, chancellor to Henry the Navigator. The stone bust in the chancel is said to be the oldest known image of Afonso Henriques, Portugal's first king. Older exhibits include prehistoric and Visigothic objects, and other eccentric displays include shrunken heads, two South American mummies and many florid pieces of sculpture.

THE BASICS

museuarqueologicodo-carmo.pt

J7

Convento do Carmo, Largo do Carmo

213 478 629

Jun–Sep Mon–Sat 10–7; Oct–May Mon–Sat 10–6. Closed public hols

Baixa-Chiado

Bus 58, 100 to Largo de Camões; tram 28; Elevador de Santa Justa

Poor

Inexpensive

HIGHLIGHTS

- Church ruins
- Shrunken heads
- Mummies
- Gothic tombs
- Bronze Age pottery
- Tiles
- Prehistoric objects

Praça do Comércio

The Arco da Rua Augusta (left) dominates the arcaded Praça do Comércio

THE BASICS

✚ K8

✉ Praça do Comércio

🚇 Terreiro do Paço/ Baixa-Chiado

🚌 All services to Praça do Comércio

♿ Good

🆓 Free

HIGHLIGHTS

- View from the waterfront
- Triumphal arch
- Arcades
- Statue of Dom José I

The majestic, spacious and theatrical square of the Praça do Comércio was built in 1785 by the Marquês de Pombal to act as a triumphal entrance to the city from the waterfront.

Gateway Locally, the square is known as the Terreiro do Paço, or Terrace of the Palace, an allusion to the 16th-century Royal Palace that stood here until it was almost completely destroyed by the 1755 earthquake. At its heart stands an equestrian statue of José I, king at the time of the 1755 earthquake, the blackened tone of its bronze giving rise to the Praça's nickname Black Horse Square. The palace's old steps still climb up from the waterfront, but today the square is dominated by the vast, 19th-century triumphal arch on its northern flank, and by ranks of imposing arcades and neoclassical government offices. In 1908, King Carlos I was assassinated together with Luis Filipe, his son and heir, in the corner of the square near Rua do Arsenal.

Today Over the past decade or so, the square has regained its role as a grand entrance to the city from the waterfront. It's been partly pedestrianized and the elegant arcades that run around the perimeter are home to cafés, bars and tempting shops. From the square, you can access the waterfront that leads to Cais do Sodré; evening, as the light fades and the ferry lights twinkle on the water, is a good time for a stroll here.

Shopping, relaxing, people-watching—it's what Lisbon's busiest square is all about

Rossio

Every city has its main square, and Lisbon's is the Rossio. It's the city's natural focus and meeting point, thronged with people and fringed with swirling traffic, a space that reflects both Lisbon's history and its tolerant present.

Turbulent past The Rossio, also known as Praça Dom Pedro IV, is Lisbon's natural focus, a large and bustling square close to one of the city's main stations, the Chiado shopping district and the Baixa. It dates from around the 13th century, though its present appearance is due mostly to the Marquês de Pombal, and 19th-century rebuilding. Between 1534 and 1820 the Inquisitors' Palace stood on the north side, and in the 16th century convicted heretics were burned in the square. The Inquisition's sentences were handed down from São Domingos church to the east, a traditional meeting place for immigrants from Guinea-Bissau and Angola.

Relaxing present Today the square is lined with cafés and shops, some with elegant facades. Many of the cafés have outside tables, the best vantage points from which to watch the world go by. The bronze statue on the 23m (75.5ft) marble pillar (1870) in the center of the square is of Dom Pedro IV; the four figures at the base represent Justice, Wisdom, Courage and Restraint—attributes ascribed to the king. The square's grandest building, the Teatro Nacional Dona Maria II (▷ 36), was built in the 1840s on the site of the Inquisitors' Palace.

THE BASICS

🚇 K7
✉ Praça Dom Pedro IV
🍴 Cafés, bars and restaurants
🚇 Rossio
🚌 All services to Rossio
♿ Poor

HIGHLIGHTS

● Cafés
● Shopfronts
● Statue of Dom Pedro IV
● Fountain
● Teatro Nacional
● Facade of Estação do Rossio (station)

Shopping in Chiado

TIP

● Check out Armazéns do Chiado (▷ 32), where you can do all your shopping under one roof, then choose somewhere on the top floor for lunch.

The much-loved Chiado neighborhood is synonymous with shopping. It has boutiques, modern department stores and some very old-fashioned and quirky specialist outlets.

District The Chiado is one of the five loosely defined districts that make up the heart of old Lisbon. Named after the poet António Ribeiro, who was nicknamed O Chiado, meaning Squeaky, it lies alongside the Baixa, spreading across the first of the slopes that rise westward to the Bairro Alto. Known primarily as a shopping district, it includes the main Largo do Chiado, and a range of streets around the Rua Garrett and Rua do Carmo. Its fashionable streets contain many luxury shops and fine old cafés, notably A Brasileira (▷ 36) in Rua

Step inside the gorgeous Café A Brasileira in the heart of Chiado to see its gilded mirrors and dark-wood panels (left); you can join poet Fernando Pessoa on a seat outside the café—perfect on a warm summer's day (middle); elaborate decoration on a facade in the Chiado district (right)

Garrett. Also here are the Teatro Nacional de São Carlos (▷ 36) opera house and the Igreja dos Mártires church, the latter built over the site of a Crusader burial ground and encampment.

Destruction On 25 August 1988 the Chiado was ravaged by fire. It is thought to have started in a store on Rua do Carmo, and devastated four blocks before being brought under control. Some 2,000 people lost their jobs, and many old buildings were gutted, including the famous Ferrari coffeehouse and the Grandella department store. Afterward the Mayor of Lisbon entrusted the reconstruction of the area to Alvaro Siza Vieira, a celebrated Portuguese architect, who rebuilt the district over the next decade to a classical plan in keeping with the surviving structures.

THE BASICS

- ✚ J8
- ✉ Streets between Rua do Carmo and Rua do Alecrim
- 🍴 Cafés, bars and restaurants
- Ⓜ Baixa-Chiado
- 🚌 758; tram 28
- ♿ Poor

More to See

AVENIDA DA LIBERDADE
Lisbon's busiest wide street, lined with grand buildings and softened by trees, scythes from the Rossio 1,500m (1,650yds) north to the Praça Marquês de Pombal and the Parque Eduardo VII.

🔲 H5–J6 ☒ Avenida da Liberdade 🚇 Restauradores, Avenida, Marquês de Pombal 🚌 711, 732

ELEVADOR DE SANTA JUSTA
This iron structure whisks you 45m (148ft) up to Rua do Carmo, giving views across the Baixa to Castelo de São Jorge, north to the central squares and south to the river.

🔲 K7 ☒ Rua Áurea to Rua do Carmo ⏰ Oct–Mar daily 7am–10pm, Jun–Sep daily 7am–11pm 🚇 Baixa-Chiado 🚌 All services to Rossio; tram 28 🖐 Inexpensive

LISBOA STORY CENTRE
lisboastorycentre.pt
This state-of-the-art multi-media attraction is a great starting place to learn about the history of Lisbon. Six zones tell the city's story down the ages through models, imagery, sound and film—be sure to take in the 4D film experience of the 1755 earthquake.

🔲 K8 ☒ Praça do Comércio 79 ☎ 211 194 099 ⏰ Daily 10–8 🚇 Terreiro de Paço 🚌 All services to Praça do Comércio 🖐 Expensive

MNAC (MUSEU NACIONAL D'ARTE CONTEMPORÂNEA DO CHIADO)
museuartecontemporanea.gov.pt
Housed in a 13th-century abbey, this museum of Portuguese painting and sculpture was refurbished in 1994. Mostly focusing on the years 1850–1950, it covers realism, romanticism, symbolism and modernism. Worth seeing are *A Sesta* by Almada Negreiros; *Lisboa e o Tejo* by Carlos Botelho; and Soares dos Reis's *O Desterrado*.

🔲 J8 ☒ Rua Serpa Pinto 4 ☎ 213 432 148/9 ⏰ Tue–Sun 10–6 🍴 Café 🚇 Baixa-Chiado 🚌 60, 208, 758; tram 28 🖐 Moderate. Free Sun and public hols until 2

NÚCLEO ARQUEOLÓGICO
ind.milleniumbcp.pt
Take an underground tour beneath the BCP bank's building in the Baixa to get a taste of the sheer age of Lisbon, and an insight into the succession of people who have lived here. This cramped and fascinating space has the remains of Roman fish tanks, an early Christian burial site and quantities of ceramics dating from the Moorish occupation.

🔲 K8 ☒ Rua dos Correeiros 21 ☎ 211 131 004 ⏰ Mon–Sat 10–12, 2–5, advance booking essential 🚇 Baixa-Chiado 🚌 All services to Rossio 🖐 Free

Tree-lined Avenida da Liberdade

Chiado District

This is not a long walk, but it can be extended to take in the maze of streets of the Bairro Alto to the north and west.

DISTANCE: 2km (1.2 miles) **ALLOW:** 2 hours with visits

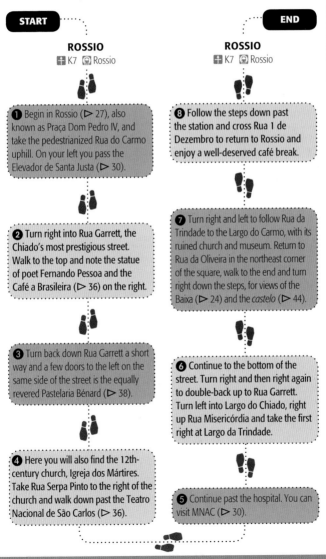

START

ROSSIO
K7 Rossio

1 Begin in Rossio (▷ 27), also known as Praça Dom Pedro IV, and take the pedestrianized Rua do Carmo uphill. On your left you pass the Elevador de Santa Justa (▷ 30).

2 Turn right into Rua Garrett, the Chiado's most prestigious street. Walk to the top and note the statue of poet Fernando Pessoa and the Café a Brasileira (▷ 36) on the right.

3 Turn back down Rua Garrett a short way and a few doors to the left on the same side of the street is the equally revered Pastelaria Bénard (▷ 38).

4 Here you will also find the 12th-century church, Igreja dos Mártires. Take Rua Serpa Pinto to the right of the church and walk down past the Teatro Nacional de São Carlos (▷ 36).

END

ROSSIO
K7 Rossio

8 Follow the steps down past the station and cross Rua 1 de Dezembro to return to Rossio and enjoy a well-deserved café break.

7 Turn right and left to follow Rua da Trindade to the Largo do Carmo, with its ruined church and museum. Return to Rua da Oliveira in the northeast corner of the square, walk to the end and turn right down the steps, for views of the Baixa (▷ 24) and the *castelo* (▷ 44).

6 Continue to the bottom of the street. Turn right and then right again to double-back up to Rua Garrett. Turn left into Largo do Chiado, right up Rua Misericórdia and take the first right at Largo da Trindade.

5 Continue past the hospital. You can visit MNAC (▷ 30).

Shopping

A CARIOCA

From behind a lovely art nouveau shopfront, A Carioca has been providing superb tea and coffee to Lisbon since 1937. The blends come from around the world.

🔳 J7 ✉ Rua da Misericórdia 9 ☎ 213 420 377 🚇 Baixa-Chiado 🚌 758; tram 28

ALBERTO SANTOS

One of the oldest handicraft shops in Lisbon (opened in the 1960s) has an assortment of genuine handmade articles displayed in large showrooms a block down from the post office.

🔳 J7 ✉ Praça dos Restauradores 64 ☎ 213 477 875 🚇 Restauradores

ANA SALAZAR

Ana Salazar is perhaps the best-known Portuguese fashion designer on the international stage. She is known primarily for her daring designs, and for special stretch fabrics. She currently has two outlets in the city. The most central is the shop on Rua do Carmo, in the Chiado.

🔳 J7 ✉ Rua do Carmo 87 ☎ 213 472 289 🚇 Rossio 🚌 All services to Rossio

ANTÓNIO TRINDADE

As well as having a fine collection of antique porcelain and religious art, this antique shop on the Rua do Alecrim specializes in antique furniture.

🔳 J8 ✉ Rua do Alecrim 79–81 ☎ 213 424 660 🚇 Baixa-Chiado

ARMAZÉNS DO CHIADO

armazensdochiado.com

A modern space over six floors, the Armazéns shopping area has high-street names and a large FNAC store, while the top floor is given over to eateries and a hotel.

🔳 J7 ✉ Rua do Carmo 2 ☎ 213 210 600 🚇 Rossio 🚌 All services to Rossio

ARTESANATO DO TEJO

Displayed inside the Lisboa Welcome Centre, Artesanato sells traditional and urban arts from the Lisbon region, from kiln-baked ceramics and paintings to woven pieces and bobbin lace.

🔳 K8 ✉ Rua do Arsenal 25 ☎ 210 312 820 🚇 Baixa-Chiado 🚌 Tram 15, 18

AZEVEDO RUA

This splendid hat shop, founded in 1886, has every type of hat you can imagine. The large range is elegantly displayed in wooden cabinets beneath a stuccoed ceiling.

🔳 K7 ✉ Praça Dom Pedro IV 69–73 ☎ 213 427 511 🚇 Rossio 🚌 All services to Rossio

CASA DE BORDADOS DE MADEIRA

Inside the Avenida Palace hotel, this shop sells embroideries from Viana do Castelo and Madeira (expensive) and the famous fishermen's sweaters from Póvoa do Varzim.

🔳 J7 ✉ Rua 10 de Dezembro 137 ☎ 213 421 447 🚇 Restauradores 🚌 All services to Avenida da Liberdade

---

SOAP BOX

Not many associate Portugal with the production of soap but the Portuguese have been hand-crafting fine soap since the 19th century. There's a huge range of old-fashioned, classic or more exotic fragrances, all long-lasting, super-foaming and gentle on the skin. But it's the exquisite art deco-style wrapping and packaging that makes the soap so special and an ideal gift to take home.

CASA HAVANEZA

Established in 1864, this shop, where tobacco is kept under optimum conditions, specializes in the very finest Cuban cigars and all manner of smoking accessories. They have another outlet in the Colombo shopping center.

🔲 J8 ✉ Largo do Chiado 24 ☎ 213 420 340 🚇 Baixa-Chiado 🚌 758; tram 28

CASA MACIEL

Lisbon is full of long-established shops: This one was founded in 1810 and has grown from a small metal-working factory into an award-winning outlet for all manner of beautifully crafted work in metal. Pieces can be made to individual designs if required.

🔲 J7 ✉ Rua da Misericórdia 63–65 ☎ 213 422 451 🚇 Rossio 🚌 758; tram 28

CASA PORTUGUESA

avidaportuguesa.com

One of the pleasures of Portugal is the highly individual and quirky approach to packaging, and the reverence for tradition of all kinds. This treasure house of a store, with its delightful and enthusiastic staff, offers the full range of nostalgic goods and design, with everything from Couto toothpaste and Encerite wax to Viana de Castelo embroidery.

🔲 J8 ✉ Rua Anchieta 11 ☎ 213 465 073 🚇 Baixa-Chiado 🚌 758; tram 28

CASA DO TURISTA

This shop does sell a selection of tacky souvenirs but it also has some tasteful regional clothing and accessories, including sweaters from Póvoa do Varzim near Oporto and scarves from the Minho.

🔲 J6 ✉ Avenida da Liberdade 159 ☎ 213 151 558 🚇 Rossio/Avenida 🚌 All services to Avenida da Liberdade

CHÁ CASA PEREIRA

casapereira.pt

This family-run shop, founded in 1930, sells a good collection of teas and coffees blended to taste. Other tempting items include vintage port and mouthwatering chocolates.

🔲 J8 ✉ Rua Garrett 38 ☎ 213 426 694 🚇 Baixa-Chiado 🚌 758; tram 28

CONFEITARIA NACIONAL

confeitarianacional.com

In business since 1829, this confectioners is renowned for its excellent almond and egg-based sweets and array of traditional cookies. For fine views across the Praça da Figueira, head to the tea-rooms on the first floor.

🔲 K7 ✉ Praça da Figueira 18B ☎ 213 424 470 🚇 Rossio

DISCOTECA AMÁLIA

Named for the Queen of Fado, Amália Rodrigues, this little record store

BAIXA-CHIADO SHOPPING

VINTAGE PORT

Vintage port—the best port—is made from the grapes of a single year only, and then only if that year's harvest has been specially declared of vintage quality. It is bottled after two to four years in the cask and then ages for at least 10 years in the bottle. Since 1974, a port must have been bottled in Portugal to be called a vintage. Late-bottled port (LBV) is a port that is not quite up to vintage standard, but is still deemed good enough to mature in the bottle rather than the cask. Typically it is bottled after about four to six years. Crucially, port that ages in the bottle matures by reduction, turning a deep red. Port that ages in the cask matures through oxidation, and turns toward amber. The longer in the cask, the lighter the shade.

specializes in fado and other Portuguese music; the English-speaking staff are delighted to pass on their knowledge.

🔲 K8 ✉ Rua Aurea 274 ☎ 213 421 485 🚇 Rossio/Baixa-Chiado 🚌 All services to Rossio

FÁBRICA SANT'ANNA

santanna.com.pt

This historic company has been Portugal's leading producer of decorated tiles, since 1741. Go to the shop on Rua do Alecrim for its beautifully decorated products, many of which are based on traditional designs. It is also possible to visit the main factory by prior arrangement.

🔲 J8 ✉ Rua do Alecrim 95–97 ☎ 213 422 537 🚌 758; tram 28

GARRAFEIRA NACIONAL

garrafeiranacional.com

Wine enthusiasts will enjoy the museum atmosphere at this wine cellar, founded in 1927. You can sample some of the finest and rarest wines, such as a very rare port wine dating from 1795.

🔲 K7 ✉ Rua de Santa Justa 18 ☎ 218 879 080 🚇 Rossio/Baixa-Chiado 🚌 All services to Praça do Comércio or Rossio

HOSPITAL DAS BONECAS

hospitaldasbonecas.com

Founded in 1830 as a dolls' hospital, this small store specializes in repairing and selling dolls. They also make delightful dolls' clothes that are sometimes bought to dress premature babies.

🔲 K7 ✉ Praça da Figueira 7 ☎ 213 428 574 🚇 Rossio

LIVRARIA BERTRAND

This charming old-fashioned shop, behind a blue-tiled facade, was founded in 1773 and is Lisbon's oldest

bookshop. It carries a good selection of illustrated books on Lisbon and Portugal.

🔲 J8 ✉ Rua Garrett 73 ☎ 213 476 122 🚇 Baixa-Chiado 🚌 758; tram 28

LORD

Behind an art deco-style facade is an atmosphere of yesteryear, where you will find a fine selection of hats and shoes suitable for the well-dressed lady and gentleman.

🔲 K8 ✉ Rua Augusta 201 ☎ 213 462 009 🚇 Rossio/Baixa-Chiado 🚌 All services to Praça do Comércio or Rossio

LUVARIA ULISSES

luvariaulisses.pt

This tiny shop is a treasure trove of gloves in every material imaginable, including silk, satin, lace, leather and cotton.

🔲 J7 ✉ Rua do Carmo 87/A ☎ 213 420 295 🚇 Rossio 🚌 All services to Rossio

MADEIRA HOUSE

madeira-house.com

This shop sells high-quality cottons, linens and gift items from the island of Madeira. It has two outlets, one in the Baixa and the other on the Avenida da Liberdade.

🔲 K8 ✉ Rua Augusta 131–135 ☎ 213 431 454 🚇 Rossio/Baixa-Chiado 🚌 All services to Praça do Comércio or Rossio

---

TILES GALORE

Azulejos have been decorating not only palaces, churches, chapels and public buildings for centuries but also the homes of Portugal, helping to waterproof against the winter rains. They are popular as souvenirs, and you can find fine hand-painted, antique and contemporary tiles to give to your friends or adorn your home.

MANUEL TAVARES

manueltavares.com

For glorious food, head to this shop in the Baixa, an institution for over 100 years. It's especially noted for the huge selection of wine, port, Madeira and brandies for sale.

🔲 K7 ✉ Rua da Betesga 1A/B ☎ 213 424 209 🚇 Rossio

PARIS EM LISBOA

parisemlisboa.pt

At this Chiado landmark you'll find quality Portuguese textile goods, from bath robes to tea towels and bed linen. The exquisite ruffled nightgowns in finest lawn are particularly tempting.

🔲 J8 ✉ Rua Garrett 77 ☎ 213 424 329 🚇 Baixa-Chiado

RETROSARIA NARDO

This haberdashers in the Baixa stocks a wide selection of buttons, ribbons, cords and threads.

🔲 K8 ✉ Rua da Conceição 62–64 ☎ 213 421 350 🚇 Baixa-Chiado

SANTOS OFICIOS

santosoficios-artesanato.pt

This shop in a restored 18th-century stable sells handmade products from around the country, including ceramics, linens and sheepskin slippers.

🔲 K8 ✉ Rua da Madalena 87 ☎ 218 872 031 🚇 Baixa-Chiado 🚌 Buses to Cossio; tram 12, 28

SARMENTO

This family-run firm has been Lisbon's most prestigious jeweler for about a hundred years. The gold, silverware and filigree are some of the most exquisite in Portugal.

🔲 K8 ✉ Rua Áurea (Rua do Ouro) 251 ☎ 213 426 774 🚇 Baixa-Chiado 🚋 Tram 28

STORYTAILORS

storytailors.pt

Designers Luís Sanchez and João Branco have set up this charming studio, where they produce tailor-made and personalized women's clothing. Inspired by the haute-couture era, their clothing shows great originality and detail.

🔲 J8 ✉ Calçada do Ferragial 8 ☎ 213 432 306 🚇 Baixa-Chiado 🚌 758; tram 28

TABACARIA MÓNACO

This tiny newsagent and tobacconist is a Lisbon landmark. Founded in 1893, it preserves a wonderful art nouveau ambience, with a lovely tiled and painted interior. It is also a good place to come for maps, guides and foreign newspapers and magazines.

🔲 K7 ✉ Praça Dom Pedro IV 21 ☎ 213 468 191 🚇 Rossio 🚌 All services to Rossio ⁉ No credit cards

TERESA ALECRIM

teresaalecrim.com

This shop is named after its owner, who produces fine high-quality embroideries created in either plain or patterned cotton. Pillowcases, sheets, towels and covers are just a few of the items she offers for sale.

🔲 K8 ✉ Rua Nova do Almada 76 ☎ 213 421 831 🚇 Baixa-Chiado 🚋 Tram 28

> ### FASHION CAPITAL
>
> From established names such as Fátima Lopes and Ana Salazar to the more recent talent of Maria Gambina and José António Tenente, Portuguese creations can be found in shops and on the catwalks of Paris, London and Barcelona, helped by fashion events such as the yearly *Moda Lisboa*, usually held in March or April.

Entertainment and Nightlife

COLISEU DOS RECREIOS

coliseulisboa.com

Hosts everything from ballet and musicals to contemporary music.

🚩 J6 ⊠ Rua Portas de Santo Antão ☎ 213 240 580; box office 18 20 🚇 Restauradores

TEATRO MUNICIPAL DE SÃO LUIZ

teatrosaoluiz.pt

This theater puts on a broad range of plays and shows, including Shakespeare.

🚩 J8 ⊠ Rua António Maria Cardoso 38 ☎ 213 257 640 🚇 Baixa-Chiado 🚌 758; tram 28

TEATRO NACIONAL DONA MARIA II

tndm.pt

There are two separate venues here

hosting classical music and drama behind a classical facade.

🚩 K7 ⊠ Praça Dom Pedro IV ☎ 213 500 800; box office 800 213 250 (toll free) 🚇 Rossio 🚌 1, 2, 31, 36, 41, all Rossio services

TEATRO NACIONAL DE SÃO CARLOS

tncs.pt

Lisbon's premier opera house, which also hosts classical concerts, ballet and theater, epitomizes 18th-century rococo splendor. It also stages works by young composers and artists in the neighboring Estúdios Victor Córdon.

🚩 J8 ⊠ Largo de São Carlos 17–21 ☎ 213 253 045 🕐 Box office: daily 1–7 🚇 Baixa-Chiado 🚌 758; tram 28

Where to Eat

PRICES

Prices are approximate, based on a 3-course meal for one person.

€€€	over €30
€€	€15–€30
€	under €15

BONJARDIM (€)

This Lisbon institution, with three outlets on the same street, is usually packed with eager diners seeking the best chicken piri-piri and chips in town. Not for nothing is it known as the Rei dos Frangos (King of Chickens), though fans also praise the steaks and other grills.

🚩 J6 ⊠ Travessa de Santo Antão 11–12 ☎ 213 427 424 🕐 Daily lunch, dinner 🚇 Restauradores

CAFÉ A BRASILEIRA (€)

The most famous of Lisbon's venerable coffeehouses in the heart of the Chiado district was once a retreat for writers and artists, notably the poet Fernando Pessoa, a statue of whom sits outside on the sidewalk. It has plenty of tables outdoors, and remains open until late, when the big beer drinkers move in.

🚩 J8 ⊠ Rua Garrett 120 ☎ 213 469 541 🕐 Daily 8am–2am 🚇 Baixa-Chiado 🚌 758; tram 28E

CAFÉ MARTINHO DA ARCADA (€–€€)

martinhodaarcada.pt

Like the Nicola (▷ 37) on the Rossio and A Brasileira (▷ this page) in the Chiado, this old coffeehouse, founded

in 1782, was a haunt of Lisbon's 19th-century literati. The adjoining restaurant is rather expensive, but the bar is good for coffee and snacks and you can sit out under the arches.

🔲 K8 ✉ Praça do Comércio 3 ☎ 218 879 259 🕐 Mon–Sat 7am–11pm 🚇 Baixa-Chiado 🚊 All services to Praça do Comércio; tram 15, 18, 25

CAFÉ NICOLA (€)

This lovely old place, dating from 1777, was a haunt for Lisbon's literary set in the 19th century and is now one of the city's most popular cafés.

🔲 K7 ✉ Rua 1 de Dezembro; entrance also at Praça Dom Pedro IV 24 ☎ 213 460 579 🕐 Mon–Sat 8am–10pm, Sun 9–7 🚇 Rossio

CAFÉ NO CHIADO (€–€€)

cafenochiado.com

This restored 18th-century building, whose colorful walls are lined with books, serves up modern European classics, with the accent on seasonality. There are outside tables.

🔲 J8 ✉ Largo do Picadeiro 10–12 ☎ 213 460 501 🕐 Mon–Thu 10am–2am, Fri–Sat 10am–3am 🚇 Baixa-Chiado 🚊 758; tram 28

CASA DO ALENTEJO (€€)

casadoalentejo.com.pt

This restaurant, in a 19th-century Franco-Arabic-style building with wonderful tiles, is a celebration of the Alentejo region as much as of the Alentejan cuisine. Dishes to try include the signature *carne de porco Alentejana*, marinated pork cooked in white wine with clams added just before serving. There is often folk dancing on Saturday.

🔲 J6 ✉ Praça Santo Antão, Rua das Portas de Santo Antão 58 ☎ 213 405 140 🕐 Daily lunch, dinner 🚇 Restauradores

CASA CHINEZA (€)

Join locals for a mid-morning stand-up snack in this beautifully decorated traditional *pastelaria* in the heart of the Baixa. The *bolos de arroz*, sweet muffins made with rice flour, are excellent.

🔲 K8 ✉ Rua da Aurea 274–78 ☎ 213 423 680 🚇 Baixa-Chiado 🚊 All Rossio services

CERVEJARIA PINÓQUIO (€)

restaurantepinoquio.pt

Established in the Baixa over 30 years ago, this is a simple, no-frills restaurant. Diners sit at long tables, service is quick and the fish fresh, brought in daily from Setúbal; so if the sea is rough, supplies run low.

🔲 J7 ✉ Praça dos Restauradores 79 ☎ 213 465 106 🕐 Daily lunch, dinner 🚇 Restauradores

CERVEJARIA TRINDADE (€–€€)

cervejariatrindade.pt

This large beer hall and *azulejo*-lined restaurant, in a former convent in the Chiado, is one of the city's oldest eating places, having been in business since 1836. The food is nothing special, but the place is a classic, and the ambiance very animated.

🔲 J7 ✉ Rua Nova da Trindade 20c ☎ 213 423 506 🕐 Daily noon–1am 🚇 Baixa-Chiado 🚊 758; tram 28

CONFEITARIA NACIONAL (€)

confeitarianacional.com

This stunning cake shop was founded in 1829, and the glass cases and painted panels bear witness to its historic origins. The first floor serves lunches and afternoon tea, while the ground floor has a takeout service.

🔲 K7 ✉ Praça da Figueira 18B ☎ 213 424 470 🕐 Daily 8–8 🚇 Rossio 🚊 All Rossio services; tram 12, 15

L'ENTRECOTE (€€)

brasserieentrecote.pt

The Chiado's smart set tend to make for this traditional but relaxed wood-paneled dining room for its faultless presentation and fine, upmarket French-influenced food. Steaks, as the name suggests, are a specialty. There is a good two-course set menu daily.

🔢 J8 ✉ Rua do Alecrim 117 ☎ 213 473 616 🕐 Daily lunch, dinner 🚇 Baixa-Chiado 🚌 758; tram 28

GAMBRINUS (€€€)

gambrinuslisboa.com

This restaurant, just off the Rossio, is one of Lisbon's most expensive. The culinary emphasis is on fish and sea-food. The setting is suitably formal, with leather chairs and a beamed ceiling. Reservations are essential.

🔢 J6 ✉ 25 Rua das Portas de Santo Antão 23 ☎ 213 421 466 🕐 Daily lunch, dinner 🚇 Restauradores

IBO (CAIS DO SODRÉ) (€€–€€€)

iborestaurante.pt

In one of the many, now converted, warehouses along the dockside, this restaurant serves excellent fresh fish and seafood used in modern and imaginative ways. There are fine views of the River Tejo.

🔢 J9 ✉ Armazem A–2, Cais do Sodré ☎ 961 332 024 🕐 Mon–Thu 12.30–3, 7–11; Fri–Sat 12.30–3, 7–1am 🚇 Cais do Sodré 🚌 15, 18

PASTELARIA BÉNARD (€)

On the Chiado's most fashionable street, Bénard's is one of Lisbon's finest cafés and pastry shops; the desserts are particularly famous.

🔢 J8 ✉ Rua Garrett 104–106 ☎ 213 473 133 🚇 Baixa-Chiado

PASTELARIA SUIÇA (€)

casasuica.pt

This café and pastry shop on Lisbon's main square competes with the historic Café Nicola (▷ 37) opposite. Both places have large and busy terraces.

🔢 K7 ✉ Praça Dom Pedro IV 96–104 ☎ 213 214 090 🚇 Rossio

SOLMAR (€€)

solmar.com.pt

With its wonderful retro 1950s décor and slick and professional service, this big and bustling restaurant is popular with *lisboetas* and visitors alike. The emphasis is on seafood and fish, but there are some meat dishes on offer.

🔢 J6 ✉ Rua das Portas de Santo Antão 108 ☎ 213 423 371 🕐 Daily lunch, dinner 🚇 Restauradores 🚌 All services to Avenida da Liberdade

TAVARES (€€€)

restaurantetavares.net

For years this glittering old-world estab-lishment, founded as a café in 1784, had a reputation as the best of Lisbon's grand restaurants. It's still excellent, offering seasonal classic dishes—try one of the tasting menus.

🔢 J8 ✉ Rua da Misericórdia 35 ☎ 213 421 112 🕐 Tue–Sat lunch, dinner 🚇 Baixa-Chiado 🚌 Tram 15, 28

TASCAS

Tascas, from the old word meaning to eat, serve no-frills cuisine—good, honest traditional fare based on recipes that use bread, pork bits and whatever the earth provides. Portions are huge and prices very reasonable. This food is known as *comida regional*, though not relating to any par-ticular region but to the country as a whole. It's the same as *comida típica*.

Mouraria-Alfama

This is the oldest part of the city, where a labyrinth of steep, narrow streets crammed with shops, restaurants and bars, Moorish architecture and splendid churches is watched over by a castle on the hill.

Top 25

5

6

Hospital
do Desterro

Rua Nova do Desterro

R Desterro

RUA DA PALMA

Benformoso

Rua da Bombarda

Rua das Olarias

Rua dos Cavaleiros

Rua M. P. de Lim

MOURAR

**Castelo de
São Jorge**

Costa do Castelo

7

R de M
São Antó

Rua de São Mame

**Santo António
de Lisboa**

**Nossa Senhora
da Conceição
Velha**

8

RUA DA ALFÂNDEG

P

**Estação Fluvial
Terreiro do Paço**

9

| 0 | | 250 m |
| 0 | | 250 yds |

Cacilhas

H   **J**   **K**

Alfama

HIGHLIGHTS

● Castelo de São Jorge
(▷ 44)
● São Miguel
● Santo Estevão
● Santa Luzia (▷ 51)
● Pátio das Flores
● Largo das Portas do Sol
● Miradouro de Santa
Luzia

TIPS

● If you do get lost, go
downhill and you will get
your bearings.
● Be aware of pickpockets.

**Tumbling down the hill from the castle to
the water, this warren of alleys and steep
cobbled streets, where flowers drip from
the balconies of tile-fronted mansions, is
redolent of the city's past.**

Hot springs There's a taste of Lisbon's Moorish
past in the labyrinth of alleyways and tiny
squares that make up the Alfama, the most
appealing of all the city's old quarters and a
delight to explore. The area takes its name from
a Moorish word, *alhama*, or fountain, a refer-
ence to the hot springs in Largo das Alcaçarías.
As a distinct enclave, however, it is much older,
probably dating back to the first Phoenician or
Roman traders who settled in the area around
present-day Castelo. Between 711 and 1147 it
became an important Moorish suburb, and later

Clockwise from far left: evocative views can be found all around this district; intricate azelujos (tiles) decorate a house; on the tourist trail in the narrow streets; fish for sale in the Rua de São Pedro; among the rooftops in old Lisbon

the home of the city's first churches. In time it became a retreat for the city's elite, losing its cachet only after the 1755 earthquake.

Sights Today, for the most part the area is an old-fashioned residential district, though gentrification of many of the once humble dwellings, restaurants and trendy shops is beginning to take the edge off its traditional appeal. The best way to see the district is to wander at random amid the streets and squares—maps are almost useless here. Streets you might try to head for include Rua de São Pedro, Rua São Miguel, Beco de Cardosa, the Pátio das Flores, Largo de São Rafael and Rua dos Remédios. Try also to take in the viewpoints at Largo das Portas do Sol and the Miradouro de Santa Luzia, which has several good cafés.

THE BASICS

🚹 L7/8–M8
✉ Around Castelo de São Jorge
🍴 Cafés, bars and restaurants
🚃 Tram 12, 28
♿ Poor
❓ Take normal precautions in poorly lit streets after dark

Castelo de São Jorge

Perched high on a hill, the castle dominates the city and offers terrific views

THE BASICS

castelosaojorge.pt

⊞ L7

✉ Rua Costa do Castelo

☎ 218 800 620

🕐 Castle: Nov–Feb daily 9–6; Mar–Oct daily 9–9 Câmara Escura: daily 10–5 (weather permitting)

🍴 Restaurant and café

🚌 737; tram 12, 28

♿ Poor

💰 Moderate (includes Câmara Escura)

HIGHLIGHTS

● Views
● Gardens
● Battlements and towers
● Parade ground

Lisbon's ancient fortress, with its breath-taking views and lovely gardens, is a shady oasis where you can sense the weight of history in the most peaceful surroundings.

Defense Lisbon's evocative castle marks the city's birthplace, the spot where Phoenician traders probably first made camp, attracted by the area's natural port, its easily defended position and its agricultural potential. Later it was fortified by the Romans, Visigoths and Moors. The defeat of the Moors, at the hands of Afonso Henriques in 1147, marked a turning point in the campaign to oust them from Portugal. Henriques took the fortress after a 17-week siege, a victory tainted by the actions of his British and French allies—supposedly Christian Crusaders—who ran amok, pillaging and murdering Moors and Christians alike.

What to see It's the site, views and grounds that give the Castelo its charm, as the original 12th-century walls and 11 towers have been much restored. You can learn more in the small museum or puzzle over the archeological site, where excavations and artifacts help trace the fortress's history. Take in the camera obscura, and the little enclave of Santa Cruz, one of the medieval jewels of the Alfama, then head to the ramparts and gardens. You'll pass a statue of Afonso Henriques en route to the terraces and pools, while the ramparts give astounding views over Lisbon and the Tagus estuary.

Fado singer in a
restaurant in the
Bairro Alto area;
Blue fado tile detail

You'll find fado sung in different parts of Lisbon but its heart lies in the Alfama, where the ancient, shadowed streets resonate with the yearning strains of Portugal's soul music, now vibrantly renewed by a new wave of performers.

The art Fado's been around for a long time (▷ 53), wonderfully expressing the Portuguese emotion of *saudade*, the yearning for the past, the distant and the unattainable. Its mid-20th-century heroine was Amália Rodrigues, whose uniquely expressive voice gained her international recognition. She died in 1999, at the end of an era when fado had lost its popularity and was associated in people's minds with the years of the Salazar dictatorship. Just a few years later, Mariza appeared on the scene, bringing new passion to fado, which she interprets by tapping into its African and Moorish roots.

Where to find it Not all performers follow the new style and performances can be perfunctory, so head for the Alfama. Even here, it's increasingly hard to find a spontaneous outburst of song, and some places are squarely aimed at tourists, but there are restaurants, bars and clubs where a tingling down your spine will tell you you're in the presence of the real thing. Among these are A Baiuca, a small, family-run restaurant whose owner is passionate about the art, and Mesa de Frades, where the singers and guitarists will help you begin to understand just what fado is all about.

THE BASICS

A Baiuca

✉ Rua de São Miguel 20

☎ 218 867 284

🕓 Thu–Mon 8pm–1am

🚃 Tram 28

♿ Poor

💶 Moderate

Mesa de Frades

✉ Rua dos Remédios 139

☎ 917 029 436

🕓 Wed–Sun 8pm–2.30am

🚃 Tram 28

♿ Poor

💶 Moderate

For more venues, see panel ▷ 53

HIGHLIGHT

● Fado vadio—spontaneous fado in non-tourist, downmarket fado bars

Feira da Ladra

The perfect pitch—flea markets in the shadow of Santa Engrácia in Campo de Santa Clara

THE BASICS

➕ M7
✉ Campo de Santa Clara
🕐 Feira da Ladra: Tue 7–1, Sat 7–4
🍴 Cafés
🚌 12, 737; tram 28
♿ Poor
❓ Watch for pickpockets

HIGHLIGHTS

● Santa Engrácia
● São Vicente de Fora
● Jardim Boto Machado

The Campo de Santa Clara area is home to two of Lisbon's best markets, the twice-weekly flea market of the Feira da Ladra, and the Mercado Municipal, a vibrant food market, while nearby are two splendid churches.

Lively market Campo de Santa Clara lies on the eastern margins of the Alfama district, one of Lisbon's most atmospheric quarters. The square and its surrounding streets are best known for their flea market, the Feira da Ladra (Thieves' Market), which takes place here on Tuesday morning and all day Saturday. The Feira's covered stalls (in the middle of the square) sell a predictable assortment of market goods—food, shoes, cheap clothes and household items—while the peripheral stalls deal in books, old postcards and bric-a-brac. Don't be fooled; genuine bargains are hard to find, but you can spend an enjoyable morning browsing here. There is another market nearby, Mercado Municipal de Santa Clara (▷ 53).

Vistas The area around Campo de Santa Clara is well worth exploring. Two of the city's more interesting churches are nearby: Santa Engrácia (▷ 50) to the southeast and São Vicente de Fora (▷ 51) to the northwest, the former completed only in 1966, the latter in 1704. São Vicente is the burial place of many of Portugal's kings and queens. At the heart of the square itself is the Jardim Boto Machado, a garden full of palms and exotic plants, with a fine view.

Museu das Artes Decorativas

This beautifully restored 17th-century palace has a stunning collection of furniture, carpets and antiques displayed in a period setting, giving the visitor a picture of upper-class Lisbon life in the 18th and 19th centuries.

Bequest Lisbon's Museum of the Decorative Arts is housed in the 17th-century palace of the Counts of Azurara, former home of Ricardo do Espírito Santo Silva (1900–55), a Portuguese philanthropist. He left the house and his private collection of art and objects to the nation in 1953. Both house and collection, run by the Espírito Santo Silva Foundation, are open to the public. The foundation also supports a series of workshops (next door) in which you can watch people practicing traditional skills such as bookbinding, wood-carving and cabinet-making.

Exquisite home Espírito Santo had exceptional taste. As a result his collection embraces some of the finest examples of Portuguese and other art and objects. The palace itself is beautiful, with its original 17th-century wooden floors, painted ceilings and panels of blue and white *azulejos* (tiles). This forms the perfect setting for the furniture, antiques, tapestries, porcelain, ceramics and rugs from Arraiolos (a central Portuguese town renowned for its exquisite carpets). Perhaps the most captivating areas are the bedrooms, complete with tiny four-poster beds, and the upstairs dining room, with its grandfather clock and fine painted ceiling.

THE BASICS

fress.pt

L7

Largo das Portas do Sol 2

218 814 600 (Mon–Fri)

Daily 10–5. Closed public hols

Café

737; tram 12, 28

Very poor: many stairs

Moderate

HIGHLIGHTS

- Palace
- Furniture
- Carpets
- Painted ceilings
- Bedrooms
- Tapestries
- Silverware
- Inlaid chess table

Sé

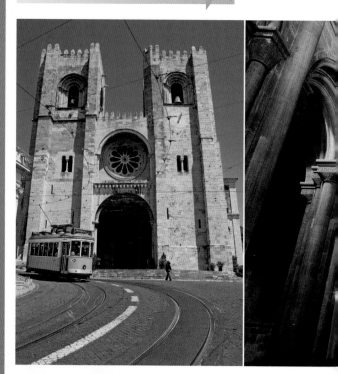

- Twin towers
- Rose window
- Baptismal font
- Bartolomeu Chapel (1324)
- *Nativity*, Joaquim Machado de Castro (1766)
- Tomb of Lopo Fernandes Pacheco
- Cloister
- Treasury
- Reliquary of St. Vincent
- Dom José I monstrance

Few sights evoke a stronger sense of Lisbon's long history than this powerful and formidable cathedral, whose ancient stone towers can be seen above the roof-tops from the Baixa and the viewpoints of the Bairro Alto.

History Lisbon's cathedral was begun around 1150, soon after Afonso Henriques, Portugal's first king, had captured the city from the Moors. It was the city's first church, and legend claims it stands on the site of a mosque. Like other Portuguese cathedrals of similar vintage—Évora, Porto, Coimbra—it has a fortress-like appearance, the result of its plain Romanesque design and the tumultuous times in which it was built, when there was still a threat from the Moors. Much of its original shell survives, notably its

Take a tram up to the impressive cathedral, in the Alfama district of the city (left); the soaring arches create an awe-inspiring sense of grandeur (right)

distinctive squat towers, which unlike the old chancel, withstood the earthquakes of 1344 and 1755, as well as the attentions of restorers.

Interior On the left as you enter the church is a font, reputedly used in 1195 to baptize St. Antony of Padua, who was born in Lisbon. The first chapel on the left is decorated with a carved Nativity scene, the work of 18th-century sculptor Joaquim Machado de Castro. More beautiful still is the tomb of Lopo Fernandes Pacheco, a courtier of Afonso IV, in the chapel on the right of the Gothic ambulatory, while the ruined 13th-century Gothic cloister has lovely sculptural fragments. According to legend, the church was protected by ravens brought here by Afonso in 1173, until the last of their descendants died in the 1970s.

THE BASICS

- L8
- Largo da Sé
- 218 876 628
- Cathedral: Mon–Sat 9–7, Sun 9–5. Cloister: daily 10–5
- Terreiro do Paço
- 737; tram 12, 28
- Poor
- Cathedral: free. Cloister: inexpensive

More to See

MUSEU E CASA DO FADO

museudofado.pt

An intriguing museum that illustrates this Portuguese passion. Learn about the history, hear the music, see how the 10-stringed Portuguese guitars are made and visit a 1940s fado house.

🔲 L8 ⊠ Largo do Chafariz de Dentro 1 ☎ 218 823 470 🕙 Tue–Sun 10–6 (last entry 5.30) 🍴 Café 🚌 28, 728, 735, 794 🎫 Inexpensive

MUSEU NACIONAL MILITAR

geira-pt/mmilitar

Following a fire and the 1755 earthquake, the complex was rebuilt as an arsenal, becoming the Artillery Museum in 1851. It houses one of the world's best artillery collections, along with displays of guns, pistols and swords. Among them are Portuguese pieces from the 16th century, and objects of French, Dutch, English, Spanish and Arab origin.

🔲 M7 ⊠ Largo do Museu da Artilharia ☎ 218 842 569 🕙 Tue–Sun 10–5

🚇 Santa Apolónia 🚌 28, 35, 745, 759, 794 🎫 Inexpensive

NOSSA SENHORA DA CONCEIÇÃO VELHA

Like Santa Luzia, this is one to enjoy from the outside. Most of the church collapsed in 1755, but the south doorway survived as a fine and rare example of the Manueline style—the ornate form of Gothic architecture associated with the reign of Manuel I (1495–1521).

🔲 K8 ⊠ Rua da Alfândega 🚌 759, 745, 790

SANTA ENGRÁCIA

patrimoniocultural.pt

This large baroque building, begun in 1682, survived the 1755 earthquake but was not completed until 1966, when the cupola was finally added. The fact that this project took 284 years to complete has led to a little Portuguese idiom—*obras de Santa Engrácia*—to mean delayed or unfinished work. The early design focuses on a balanced Greek cross with four

The Museu Nacional Militar

towers and curving arms, and was influenced by new departures in contemporary Italian baroque architecture. The result is a slightly austere and over-precise building, well suited to its memorial function.

🖽 M7 ☒ Campo de Santa Clara ☎ 218 854 820 🕓 Tue–Sun 10–5 🚌 12, 704, 737, 781; tram 28 💷 Inexpensive. Free Sun

SANTA LUZIA

The exterior walls of this church are covered in *azulejos* depicting Lisbon before and after the earthquake of 1755, and its garden is laid out as a charming viewpoint, the Miradouro de Santa Luzia.

🖽 L8 ☒ Largo de Santa Luzia 🚌 737; tram 28

SANTO ANTÓNIO DE LISBOA

This little church stands on the site of the house where St. Antony was born in 1195. Built after the 1755 earthquake, it contains paintings by Pedro de Carvalho. The square in which the church sits is called Santo António de Sé because the church is immediately in front of the cathedral. A small museum displays objects related to the saint's life.

🖽 L8 ☒ Largo de Santo António de Sé 24 ☎ Museum: 218 860 447 🕓 Church: daily 8–7.30. Museum: Tue–Sun 10–1, 2–6. Closed public hols 🚌 737; tram 28 💷 Church: free. Museum: inexpensive

SÃO VICENTE DE FORA

patrimoniocultural.pt

São Vicente was built between 1582 and 1627 on the site of a 12th-century church erected to commemorate the Crusaders' victory over the Moors. The present church was constructed during Portugal's period of subjugation to the Spanish, and was the work of the Italian Filippo Terzi. His cupola, felled by the 1755 earthquake, was replaced by a more modest dome, though the nave survives, with its coffered vault and baroque altar.

🖽 M7 ☒ Largo de São Vicente ☎ 218 244 400 🕓 Tue–Sat 9–5, Sun 9–12.30 🚌 12, 737; tram 28 💷 Church: free. Monastery: moderate

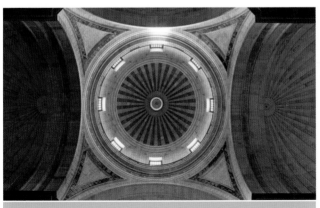

Detail of the baroque-inspired dome of the church of Santa Engrácia

Around the Alfama

The best way to explore the Alfama district, with its maze of tiny streets, is on foot. Here you will really experience old Lisbon.

DISTANCE: 2.5km (1.5 miles) **ALLOW:** 2 hours

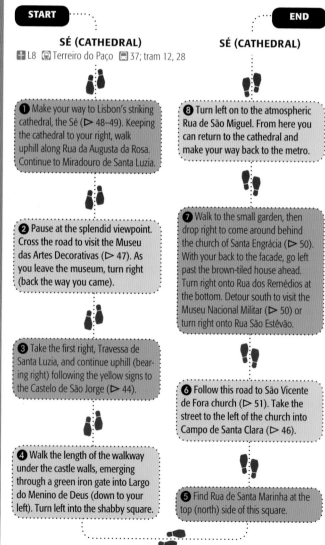

START

SÉ (CATHEDRAL)
L8 Terreiro do Paço 37; tram 12, 28

① Make your way to Lisbon's striking cathedral, the Sé (▷ 48–49). Keeping the cathedral to your right, walk uphill along Rua da Augusta da Rosa. Continue to Miradouro de Santa Luzia.

② Pause at the splendid viewpoint. Cross the road to visit the Museu das Artes Decorativas (▷ 47). As you leave the museum, turn right (back the way you came).

③ Take the first right, Travessa de Santa Luzia, and continue uphill (bearing right) following the yellow signs to the Castelo de São Jorge (▷ 44).

④ Walk the length of the walkway under the castle walls, emerging through a green iron gate into Largo do Menino de Deus (down to your left). Turn left into the shabby square.

END

SÉ (CATHEDRAL)

⑧ Turn left on to the atmospheric Rua de São Miguel. From here you can return to the cathedral and make your way back to the metro.

⑦ Walk to the small garden, then drop right to come around behind the church of Santa Engrácia (▷ 50). With your back to the facade, go left past the brown-tiled house ahead. Turn right onto Rua dos Remédios at the bottom. Detour south to visit the Museu Nacional Militar (▷ 50) or turn right onto Rua São Estêvão.

⑥ Follow this road to São Vicente de Fora church (▷ 51). Take the street to the left of the church into Campo de Santa Clara (▷ 46).

⑤ Find Rua de Santa Marinha at the top (north) side of this square.

Shopping

CONSERVEIRA DE LISBOA

conserveiradelisboa.pt

Established in the 1930s, this old-fashioned shop, with its original décor, sells nothing but the finest quality tinned fish—sardines, tuna, squid, anchovies and anything else you can think of.

🔁 L8 ✉ Rua dos Bacalhoeiras 34 ☎ 218 864 009 🚌 737; tram 12, 28

FÁBRICA DE CÉRAMICA VIÚVA LAMEGO

viuvalamego.com

This factory dates back to 1879. The factory shop, adorned with tiles on its exterior, sells mainly copies of traditional designs, together with a small selection of pottery. It will also take orders for bespoke tiles.

🔁 K5 ✉ Largo do Intendente 25 ☎ 218 852 408 🚇 Intendente 🚌 708; tram 28

MERCADO MUNICIPAL DE SANTA CLARA

This vibrant food market sells just about every type of produce and has some excellent eating opportunities on its upper level.

🔁 M7 ✉ Campo de Santo Clara 🚌 12, 34; tram 28

Entertainment and Nightlife

CLUBE DE FADO

clube-de-fado.com

A great venue, which puts on quality *fado* performances in a colonnaded arched hall., this is the place to hear genuine performances from *fadistas* such as Miguel Capucho. It's not cheap, but you can eat at the bar.

🔁 L8 ✉ Rua São João da Praça 94 ☎ 218 852 704 🕐 Daily 8pm–2am 🚌 737; tram 12, 28

LUX

luxfragil.com

Over two floors in a riverside warehouse, with a cool retro interior, DJs play a mix of dance and mainstream music to a stylish crowd. When the noise gets too much, chill out on the terrace.

🔁 M7 ✉ Avenida Infante D. Henrique, Armazém A, Cais da Pedra, Santa Apolónia ☎ 218 820 890 🕐 Tue–Sat 10pm–6am 🚌 745, 759, 794

PARREIRINHA DE ALFAMA

parreirinhadealfama.com

Another of the city's more venerable clubs, this has some of the greatest names in *fado*. Both the cover charge and food prices are lower than those of its rivals. No dancing.

🔁 M8 ✉ Beco do Espírito Santo 1, off Largo do Chafariz de Dentro ☎ 218 868 209 🕐 Daily 8pm–2am 🚌 737; tram 28

HISTORY OF FADO

Lisbon and Coimbra are the two great cities of fado—a melancholy form of traditional singing accompanied by guitar. Passion, fate and regrets are the main themes. It may originate from African slave songs, or have Moorish roots. In Lisbon, the singer (*fadista*) is nearly always a woman, and is accompanied by one or two impassive male guitarists. Coimbra fado is sung by men and has a less heart-rending quality.

Where to Eat

PRICES

Prices are approximate, based on a 3-course meal for one person.

€€€   over €30
€€   €15–€30
€   under €15

BICA DO SAPATO (€€–€€€)

bicadosapato.com

This classy warehouse conversion has river views and a great terrace. The food lives up to the surroundings too, with a sushi bar and a menu focusing on modern interpretations of dishes using the best of Portuguese produce.

🔲 M8 ✉ Avenida Infante D. Henrique, Armazém B, Cais da Pedra, Santa Apolónia ☎ 218 810 320 🕓 Tue–Sun lunch, dinner, Mon dinner only. Sushi bar: Mon–Sat dinner only 🚌 745, 759, 794

CAFÉ CERCA MOURA (€)

Close to the Miradouro de Santa Luzia in Largo das Portas do Sol, this café has fine views of the River Tejo and a good selection of snacks and drinks.

🔲 L8 ✉ Largo das Portas do Sol 4 ☎ 218 874 859 🕓 Daily noon–2am 🚌 Tram 12E, 28E

CASANOVA (€€)

This restaurant offers good-value Italian food with a fun atmosphere—diners attract the waiter by turning on the red light above the table. Opt for pizza cooked fresh in the wood-fired oven, or for a more hearty meal try a slow-cooked bean dish. No reservations, but you shouldn't have to wait long for a place at the shared tables.

🔲 M8 ✉ Avenida Infante D. Henrique, Cais da Pedra, Armazém 7 Loja B ☎ 218 877 532 🕓 Tue–Sun 12.30–1am 🚌 28, 35, 745, 759, 794

LAUTASCO (€€)

This Alfama restaurant is popular with locals and visitors, who come here not so much for the simple Portuguese fare but for the delightful atmospheric courtyard.

🔲 L8 ✉ Beco do Azinhal 7A, off Rua de São Pedro-Largo Chafariz de Dentro ☎ 218 860 173 🕓 Mon–Sat lunch, dinner 🚌 745, 759, 794

MALMEQUER-BEMMEQUER (€–€€)

A welcoming choice in an atmospheric street in the Alfama district. Plenty of basic Portuguese dishes.

🔲 L8 ✉ Rua São Miguel 23–25, Largo de São Miguel ☎ 218 876 535 🕓 Wed–Sun lunch, dinner, Tue dinner only 🚌 737; tram 28

VIA GRAÇA (€€€)

restauranteviagraca.com

Set in a romantic spot right near the Miradouro de Graça, this highly rated restaurant is housed in what appears from the exterior to be an unattractive modern building. Come inside, though, and enjoy some of the finest views in Lisbon, while you eat good modern Portuguese cuisine.

🔲 L6 ✉ Rua Damasceno Monteiro 9-B ☎ 218 870 830 🕓 Mon–Fri lunch, dinner, Sat–Sun dinner 🚌 Tram 28

HALF PORTIONS

Servings tend to be generous in Portugal, and many soups and starters are rich and filling enough to be meals in themselves. If you can't manage whole portions, ask if you can have a half portion, or share one serving between two—many restaurants are happy to serve smaller portions, especially those in the lower price range, and some even list half portions on the menu.

Bairro Alto/ The West

Bairro Alto stands high above the city, a bohemian area with a vibrant nightlife. On the western slopes lie Estrela, crowned by its basilica; the parliament district of São Bento; and Lapa, which runs into Santos and the Alcântara.

Top 25

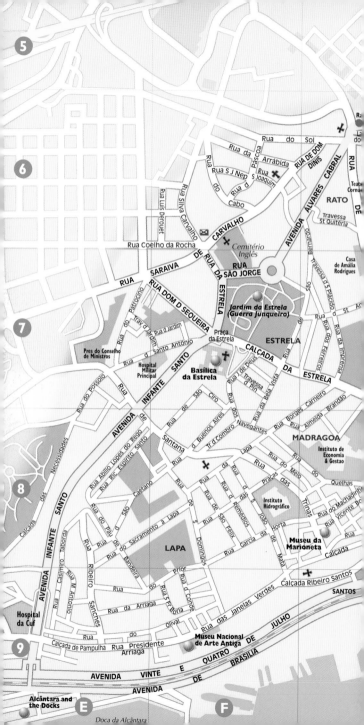

RUA DO Vale do Pereiro

Rua Barata Salgueiro

RUA DO SALITRE

RUA DA ESCOLA

Museu M João da Silva

Rua N São Mamede

Rua Cec. do Arco

Rua Gustavo de Matos

Museu Nacional História Natural e da Ciência

Jardim Botânico

Teatros

Universidade Internacional

Praça da Alegria

POLITÉCNICA

Rua da Imprensa Nacional

Rua N Portugal

Rua M Portugal

Rua Manuel Bernardes

Rua N Bernardes

Rua de S. Marçal

Rua da Sequeira

Rua Cec. de Sousa

Rua Mãe de Água

Rua St Antonio Gloria

Rua das Taipas

Rua da Gloria

Praça do Principe Real

RUA DOM PEDRO V

RUA S. P. ALCANTARA

Miradouro de São Pedro de Alcântara

Elevador da Gloria

Travessa C Soure

BENTO

Rua D. Pedro V

Rua d Palmeira

Rua Eduardo Coelho

Rua d Jasm.

Travessa da Boa Hora

Rua Nova do Loureiro

Rua da Vinha

Rua da Rosa

Travessa da Queimada

Igreja de São Roque

RUA D MISERICÓRDIA

Praça de São Bento

alácio e São Bento

Assembleia da República

Rua da Quintinha

Trav St Ter

Rua Academia Ciências

Academia das Ciências de Lisboa

Rua do Século

Rua

T do Poço da Cidade

Travessa dos Fiéis de Deus

BAIRRO ALTO

Rua das Gáveas

Trav. de Arrochela

Rua Cruz dos

T do Paçço da Cidade

AVENIDA DE DOM CARLOS I

Rua de São Bento

Rua da Vale

Rua da P de São Bento

Rua d Poço d Negros

S Catarina

Calçada do Combro

Rua d Sol

Rua do Alcaide

Rua de Sta Catarina

Rua d Almada

Rua da Bica D B

Elevador da Bica

Rua das Chagas

R d H Seca

Rua d Loreto

Praça L de Camões

D O A L E C R I M

Esperança

de Abrantes

Rua da Boa Vista

Rua Tomás Fernandes

Rua Inst. Industrial

Rua das Flores

Rua da Emenda

Rua da Ataíde

Marquês Largo V Damásio

Largo d Santos

Rua d Boa

Rua do Duro

Dom

Luis I

Rua dos Ferreiros

Rua da Boa

Rua d Ribeira

Mercado da Ribeira

Rua Nova do Carvalho

RUA DO ALECRIM

Praça D da Terceira

AVENIDA VINTE E QUATRO DE JULHO

Praça de Dom Luis I

Cais do Sodré

AVENIDA DE BRASÍLIA

CAIS DO SODRÉ

Cais do Sodré

Estação Fluvial Cais do Sodre

Tejo

0   250 m
0   250 yds

Almada/Cacilhas

G   H   J

Bairro Alto

TOP
25

A decorated house (left) and a typical street in the Bairro Alto (right)

THE BASICS

➕ H7–H8

✉ Streets enclosed by Rua da Boa Vista, Rua da Misericórdia, Rua do Século and Rua Dom Pedro V

🍴 Many bars and cafés

🚇 Baixa-Chiado or Restauradores/Elevador da Glória

🚋 Tram 28

♿ Very poor

HIGHLIGHTS

● Elevador da Glória
● Solar do Vinho do Porto
● Miradouro de São Pedro de Alcântara
● Rua de Atalaia (shopping)
● Rua do Diário de Notícias (shopping)

Traditionally the bohemian haunt of students, artists and writers, the narrow cobbled streets of the Bairro Alto, home of traditional fado singing, should not be missed on any visit to the city.

Nightlife The Bairro Alto, or Upper Town, is one of Lisbon's liveliest and most distinctive quarters, and one of the five loosely defined areas that make up the heart of the old city. Traditionally a working-class area, it was first developed in the 1500s, when merchants settled here. It was hardly damaged by the 1755 earthquake, and rises in a close-knit grid of 16th-century streets up the steep slopes west of the Chiado and Baixa districts. During the day its quiet corners are filled with the sort of evocative scenes you find all over Lisbon—washing strung from the windows and children playing in the streets. As night falls, the restaurants and bars open and by 10pm the strains of fado can be heard as the area becomes the principal focus of Lisbon's nightlife.

Sights Exploring the Bairro's streets is worth doing for its own sake, but some sights deserve special attention. These include the Elevador da Glória, a funicular built in 1885, which will save you a lot of climbing by carrying you up from the Baixa district below. Other sights are the Solar do Vinho do Porto, run by the Port Wine Institute, and the Igreja de São Roque (▷ 60–61). The Miradouro de São Pedro de Alcântara (▷ 65) has some fine views over the city.

The austere Basílica da Estrela holds some superb treasures within its walls

Basílica da Estrela

Set high on a hill, this ebullient master-piece, a symbol of the city, perfectly fuses the architectural flamboyance of an age of wealth and power with the intellectual austerity that existed alongside.

Offering Like the Palácio de Fronteira, the Basílica da Estrela lies some way from the heart of the city—2km (1.2 miles) to the west of the Bairro Alto—but it is more than worth the effort required to see it, and you can combine a trip here with a visit to the Jardim da Estrela (Jardim Guerra Junqueiro), one of the city's most beautiful gardens (▷ 64). The basilica, a monumental white edifice with an impressive dome, was founded by Dona Maria I in 1779 as a votive offering for the birth of a son, José. It is a neoclassical masterpiece.

Impressive The church's architects, Mateus Vicente and Reinaldo Manuel, were influenced by the Palácio-Convento at Mafra (▷ 106), a building whose main attribute is size. Size is also the basilica's defining feature, the austere interior a cavernous expanse of marble. To the left of the high altar lies the tomb of Dona Maria I, who died in Brazil in 1816 and whose body was returned to Portugal for burial six years later. Don't miss the Sala do Presépio, a room housing a 500-piece Christmas crib carved from cork, before tackling the 140 stone steps to the dome, where you can take in the huge views to the west or peer down into the church.

THE BASICS

- ✚ F7
- ✉ Largo da Estrela
- ☎ 213 960 915
- ◷ Daily 8–7
- Ⓡ Rato
- 🚍 713, 773; tram 25, 28
- ♿ Poor
- 💲 Free

HIGHLIGHTS

- ● Facade
- ● Twin towers
- ● Tomb of Dona Maria I
- ● Views from the dome
- ● Jardim da Estrela

Igreja de São Roque

HIGHLIGHTS

- Painted wooden ceiling
- Capela de São Roque
- Tile decoration
- Capela de São João Baptista
- Mosaics

TIP

- Beside the church is the Museu de Arte Sacra, which has a rich collection of paintings, embroidery and ecclesiastical plates.

The Igreja de São Roque has one of the most extravagantly decorated interiors in Lisbon. The ceilings of the church are filled with paintings and the chapels groan under the weight of gold, gilt, marble and other precious materials.

Lavish interior Little in the plain facade of this church prepares you for the decorative glory within. Commissioned by the Jesuits, it dates from 1565 and was the work of Filippo Terzi, also responsible for the church of São Vicente across the city. His original facade fell victim to the 1755 earthquake, but the interior was saved, according to popular belief, by the personal intervention of St. Roch (São Roque). Inside, the *trompe l'œil* painting on the ceiling is a triumph, while each of the eight chapels

The magnificently decorated interior of the Church of São Roque, built in the 16th century following Filippo Terzi's plans, displays a wealth of riches and adornments

lining the nave is a decorative masterpiece. The third chapel on the right, the Capela de São Roque, has some of the finest *azulejos* (tiles) in the city, including the work of Francisco de Matos from 1584, his only known commission.

Chapel The fourth chapel on the left, the Capela de São João Baptista, has been called the most expensive chapel for its size ever built. Commissioned in 1742 by João V, it was designed by Vanvitelli, the papal architect, and built in Rome. It was blessed by Pope Benedict XIV before being shipped to Lisbon, where its ensemble of precious materials—amethyst, ivory, porphyry and Carrara marble among others—was reassembled. Note the chapel's "paintings", which are not really paintings but extraordinarily detailed mosaics.

THE BASICS

- J7
- Largo Trindade Coelho
- 213 235 283; museum 213 235 444
- Museum: Apr–Sep Mon 2–7, Tue–Sun 10–7; Oct–Mar Mon 2–6, Tue–Sun 10–6. Closed public hols. Church: daily 8.30–5
- Baixa-Chiado
- 758; Elevador da Glória
- Poor
- Church: free. Museum: inexpensive; free on Sun and public hols

Museu Nacional de Arte Antiga

HIGHLIGHTS

● *Adoration of St. Vincent*, Nuno Gonçalves
● Cook Triptych, Grão Vasco
● *Annunciation*, Frei Carlos
● *Temptation of St. Antony*, Hieronymus Bosch
● *Madonna and Child*, Hans Memling
● *St. Jerome*, Albrecht Dürer
● *St. Augustine*, Piero della Francesca

TIPS

● Pick up a leaflet to aid your visit.
● Take a lunch break in the pleasant café.

The Museu Nacional de Arte Antiga, beautifully presented in a 17th-century palace, traces the history of Portugal and its way of life through a dazzling collection of paintings, sculpture, furniture and textiles from Portugal and the world.

Collection The National Museum of Ancient Art contains one of Portugal's finest art collections, and ranks second only to the Gulbenkian among Lisbon's galleries and museums. The collection of paintings traces the development of Portuguese art from the 11th century onward and also includes work by several major European artists. There is also a wealth of decorative art and silverware, notably Italian ceramics, ecclesiastical vestments, Flemish tapestries, and a monstrance from the Mosteiro

(▷ 86–87) in Belém that was reputedly made from the first gold brought back from the Indies by Vasco da Gama. Also worth seeing are a chapel, preserved from a convent previously on the site, and the Namban screens, which depict the arrival of the Portuguese in Japan in 1543.

Adoration The museum's most famous painting by far is an altarpiece, the *Painéis de São Vicente de Fora*, or *Adoration of St. Vincent*, thought to be painted by Nuno Gonçalves between 1465 and 1470. It was discovered in a defunct Lisbon church in 1882. Its six panels portray around 60 figures paying homage to St. Vincent, Lisbon's patron saint, who is depicted twice. Other treasures include works by Grão Vasco, Frei Carlos, Memling, Holbein, Dürer, Raphael and Velázquez.

THE BASICS

museudearteantiga.pt

⊞ F9

✉ Rua das Janelas Verdes

☎ 213 912 800

🕐 Tue–Sun 10–6

🍴 Small bar and restaurant

🚌 713, 714, 727, 732; tram 15, 18, 25

🚉 Santos (Cascais line)

♿ Very good: lift, small steps

💰 Moderate

More to See

ALCÂNTARA AND THE DOCKS

Lisbon's docklands crouch beneath the elegant span of the Ponte 25 de Abril, which was opened in 1966. Utilitarian by day, at night and at weekends the area buzzes, largely due to the re-development of the surrounding warehouses, now devoted to eating, drinking and clubbing. From the Doca de Santo Amaro you can pick up a riverside path that runs all the way to Belém.

➕ E9 ✉ Alcântara 🚇 Cascais line to Alcântara 🚌 12, 28, 714, 738, 742; tram 15, 18

JARDIM BOTÂNICO

Spread across a slope just above Avenida da Liberdade, this botanical garden should not be missed. It was laid out in 1873 by the Faculty of Sciences of the University of Lisbon. Mazes of little paved paths wind downhill past masses of exotic plants and trees, all clearly marked. The Rua da Alegria entrance closes early during the week and is closed on weekends.

➕ H6 ✉ Rua Escola Politécnica 58-Rua da Alegria ☎ 213 921 800 🕐 Apr–Oct Mon–Fri 9–8, Sat–Sun 10–8; Nov–Mar Mon–Fri 9–6, Sat–Sun 10–6 🚇 Rato 🚌 758 💷 Inexpensive

JARDIM GUERRA JUNQUEIRO

This park is better known as the Jardim da Estrela, after the Basílica da Estrela (▷ 59). It is popular with families and has playgrounds, shady patches and a small duck-dotted lake (with adjacent café), which is the park's natural focus. There is also a wrought-iron gazebo, and on summer afternoons there are occasional brass-band concerts.

➕ F7 ✉ Calçada da Estrela 🕐 7am–midnight 🍴 Café 🚇 Rato 🚌 709, 720, 738; tram 25, 28 💷 Free

LX FACTORY

lxfactory.com

A huge ex-textile factory houses one of Lisbon's most vibrant creative spaces, the stylish LX Factory. There are studios, galleries and workshops and frequent shows, live music and

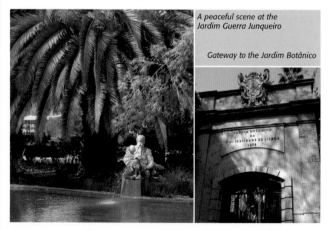

A peaceful scene at the Jardim Guerra Junqueiro

Gateway to the Jardim Botânico

screenings. Head here on Sundays when there's a flea market.

🚹 C9 ⊠ Rua Rodrigues Faria 103 ☎ 213 143 399 ⊙ See website for opening times and events 🚇 Cascais line to Alcântara 🚍 12, 28, 714, 738, 742; tram 15, 18

MERCADO DA RIBEIRA

Lisbon's oldest market has undergone a major update in the past few years, emerging as a chic and vibrant food hall. The old fruit, fish and vegetable stalls do brisk morning business, and upstairs the scent of flowers overwhelms, but at lunchtime, stalls representing Lisbon's top chefs and food outlets get going, making this a top choice for eating and people-watching.

🚹 J8–J9 ⊠ Avenida 24 Julho ☎ 212 244 980 ⊙ Fish and produce market: Mon–Sat 6–2; food stalls: Sun–Wed 10am–midnight, Thu–Sat 10am–2am 🚇 Cais do Sodré 🚍 713, 714, 727, 732; tram 15, 18

MIRADOURO DE SÃO PEDRO DE ALCÂNTARA

Perched on the edge of the Bairro Alto, this belvedere offers sweeping views of the Rossio and Baixa below. Part of the fun here is to travel the old Elevador da Glória, built in 1885.

🚹 J7 ⊠ Rua São Pedro de Alcântara 🚇 Restauradores 🚍 758; Glória elevador

MUSEU DO CENTRO CIENTÍFICO E CULTURAL DE MACAU

cccm.pt

This is the only museum outside China to focus on Portugal's former colony of Macau, handed back to China in 1999. The ground floor details the development of trade routes to Macau and China, with model boats, maps, journals and audio displays. Upstairs, you can admire the superb collection of Chinese ceramics, porcelain, silverware, intricately carved ivory boxes and opium pipes.

🚹 Off map C9 ⊠ Rua do Junqueira 30 ☎ 213 617 570 ⊙ Tue–Sun 10–6 🚇 Cascais line to Alcântara 🚍 12, 28, 714, 738, 742; tram 25, 18 📳 Moderate

MUSEU DA MARIONETA

museudamarioneta.pt

Housed in the beautifully restored 17th-century Convento das Bernardas, this fascinating museum displays indigenous puppets from Japan, Thailand, Burma and Indonesia. There are also occasional puppet shows.

🚹 G8 ⊠ Rua da Esperança 146 ☎ 213 942 810 ⊙ Tue–Sun 10–1, 2–6 🚍 713, 714, 727; tram 25 📳 Inexpensive

MUSEU DO ORIENTE

museudooriente.pt

A vast converted warehouse is home to this museum, devoted to the cultural ties between Portugal and its former colonies in India and the Far East. It's owned by the Orient Foundation, whose collections include superb Chinese porcelain, ivory carvings and beautiful screens. Upstairs, the focus is on gods of Asia, with effigies, costumes and religious artifacts from Bali, Japan, Thailand, Indonesia and Vietnam.

🚹 D9 ⊠ Avenida Brasília 352, Alcântara ☎ 213 585 200 ⊙ Tue–Thu, Sat–Sun 10–6, Fri 10–10 🚇 Cascais line to Alcântara 🚍 12, 28, 714, 738, 742; tram 25, 18 📳 Moderate

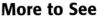

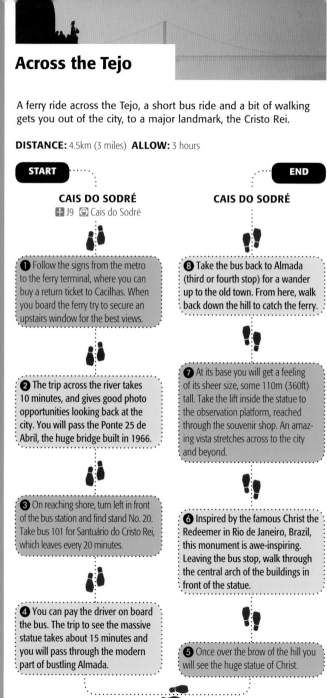

Across the Tejo

A ferry ride across the Tejo, a short bus ride and a bit of walking gets you out of the city, to a major landmark, the Cristo Rei.

DISTANCE: 4.5km (3 miles) **ALLOW:** 3 hours

START

CAIS DO SODRÉ
⊞ J9 ⓜ Cais do Sodré

END

CAIS DO SODRÉ

❶ Follow the signs from the metro to the ferry terminal, where you can buy a return ticket to Cacilhas. When you board the ferry try to secure an upstairs window for the best views.

❷ The trip across the river takes 10 minutes, and gives good photo opportunities looking back at the city. You will pass the Ponte 25 de Abril, the huge bridge built in 1966.

❸ On reaching shore, turn left in front of the bus station and find stand No. 20. Take bus 101 for Santuário do Cristo Rei, which leaves every 20 minutes.

❹ You can pay the driver on board the bus. The trip to see the massive statue takes about 15 minutes and you will pass through the modern part of bustling Almada.

❽ Take the bus back to Almada (third or fourth stop) for a wander up to the old town. From here, walk back down the hill to catch the ferry.

❼ At its base you will get a feeling of its sheer size, some 110m (360ft) tall. Take the lift inside the statue to the observation platform, reached through the souvenir shop. An amazing vista stretches across to the city and beyond.

❻ Inspired by the famous Christ the Redeemer in Rio de Janeiro, Brazil, this monument is awe-inspiring. Leaving the bus stop, walk through the central arch of the buildings in front of the statue.

❺ Once over the brow of the hill you will see the huge statue of Christ.

Shopping

AMOREIRAS

amoreiras.com

Lisbon's first mall is in the Torres das Amoreiras north of the city. This distinctive building was designed by Tomás Taveira, one of Portugal's leading architects. It contains a hotel, 10 cinemas, more than 70 cafés and restaurants, and some 350 shops. Most stay open until late, seven days a week.

📍 F5 ✉ Avenida Engenheiro Duarte Pacheco ☎ 213 810 200 🚌 711, 713, 723, 748, 753, 774, 783, 202

CAZA DAS VELLAS DO LORETO

cazavellasloreto.com.pt

This beautiful old store was founded in 1789 to manufacture the candles traditionally used to celebrate religious festivals and occasions such as christenings and confirmation. They still make them, but you can also find wonderful scented candles, candles for dining tables and all sorts of accessories.

📍 J8 ✉ Rua do Loreto 53 ☎ 213 425 387 🚇 Baixa-Chiado

DEPOSITO DA MARINHA GRANDE

dmg.com.pt

These shops are outlets for Marinha Grande's own reasonably priced glass and china. The firm is long established, and its Atlantis glass is well known in Portugal.

📍 G6 ✉ Rua de São Bento 234–242 ☎ 213 963 234 🚇 Rato, Baixa-Chiado 🚌 706, 727, 773; tram 25, 28

EL DORADO

Come here for secondhand vintage clothing, mainly from the 1950s, 1960s and 1970s. It also sells records.

📍 J7 ✉ Rua do Norte 23–25 ☎ 213 423 935 🚇 Baixa-Chiado

FÁTIMA LOPES

fatima-lopes.com

One of Portugal's most successful designers, Fátima Lopez sells cutting-edge styles in sleek body-hugging fabrics.

📍 J7 ✉ Rua da Atalaia 36 ☎ 213 240 546 🚇 Baixa-Chiado

LIVRARIA LEYA NA BUCHHOLZ

This pleasantly jumbled shop over three floors sells a range of English-language books (as well as an excellent range of Portuguese titles), and is one of the few outlets to sell Portuguese folk and other ethnic music.

📍 H5 ✉ Rua Duque de Palmela 4 ☎ 213 170 580 🚇 Marquês de Pombal

PRÍNCIPE REAL

This prestigious firm produces and sells some of the loveliest table linens, cottons and other fabrics in the city. Royalty and all manner of rich and famous clients have patronized the shop. Sheets and tablecloths are good buys, and prices are not as outrageous as you might expect.

📍 H6 ✉ Rua da Escola Politécnica 12–14 ☎ 213 465 945 🚌 758

COCKERELS

It's hard to avoid the ubiquitous Barcelos Cock painted pottery and wooden models, based on a tale told across the Iberian peninsula. A pilgrim heading for Santiago de Compostela was unjustly accused of theft on leaving Barcelos. Despite pleading innocence, he was found guilty and sentenced to death. Looking at the roast cockerel served for the judge's dinner, he invoked the help of St. James, saying that if he were innocent the dead cock would crow. This it promptly did and the man was released.

BAIRRO ALTO/THE WEST SHOPPING

Entertainment and Nightlife

ADEGA DO MACHADO

adegamachado.pt

This was once one of the oldest and most revered of all the fado clubs, and you can still experience fado and folk dancing in traditional costume there, albeit rather touristy these days.

🕂 J7 ⊠ Rua do Norte 91 ☎ 213 422 282 🕔 Tue–Sun 8.30pm–2am 🚇 Baixa-Chiado 🚌 758; tram 28

ADEGA DO RIBATEJO

Ribatejo has fado performances by paid singers and sometimes the cooks or the management take part.

🕂 J7 ⊠ Rua Diário de Notícias 23 ☎ 213 468 343 🕔 Mon–Sat 8pm–12.30am 🚇 Baixa-Chiado 🚌 758; tram 28

ARCADAS DO FAIA

ofaia.com

You are guaranteed to hear good authentic fado at this Bairro Alto spot. It also serves excellent traditional Portuguese cooking.

🕂 J7 ⊠ Rua da Barroca 54–56 ☎ 213 426 742 🕔 Mon–Sat 8pm–2am 🚌 758; tram 28

A SEVERA

asevera.com

Named after a legendary 19th-century gypsy *fadista*, A Severa attracts big names in fado and charges high prices.

🕂 J7 ⊠ Rua das Gáveas 51–61 ☎ 213 428 314 🕔 Thu–Tue 8pm–3am 🚇 Baixa-Chiado 🚌 758; tram 28

BLUES CAFÉ

A former warehouse on the Doca de Alcântara, in the waterfront district, this is now a bar-club-restaurant that serves Cajun food. Live blues is performed two or three nights a week, and there's dance music at the weekend.

🕂 E9 ⊠ Rua da Cintura do Porta de Lisboa, Armazen H, Navez ☎ 213 957 085 🕔 Tue–Sat 8.30pm–4am 🚊 Alcântara Mar (Cascais line from Cais do Sodré) 🚌 28, 727; tram 15

CAFÉ LUSO

cafeluso.pt

Housed in the cellar of a 17th-century palace, Café Luso is one of the most renowned fado and folklore restaurants in Lisbon. Many major artists have performed here.

🕂 J7 ⊠ Travessa da Queimada 10 ☎ 213 422 281 🕔 Daily 🚇 Baixa-Chiado 🚌 758; tram 28

CINCO LOUNGE

cincolounge.com

Atmospheric lighting and huge sofas are the keynote design features at this very popular and high-end New York-style cocktail bar, where the friendly bar staff will expertly knock up any of the impressive hundred plus combinations on offer.

🕂 H7 ⊠ Rua Ruben A Leitão 17 ☎ 213 424 033 🕔 Daily 9pm–2am 🚇 Rato 🚌 758

WHERE TO GO

For years you had to go no farther than the streets of the Bairro Alto to find a good night out. These days many of the best bars and clubs lie farther afield. You'll find clubs on and around the Avenida da 24 de Julho (along the waterfront west of Cais do Sodré), the Alcântara district (notably the fast-growing and increasingly fashionable Doca do Santo Amaro, also on the waterfront, and using refurbished warehouses), and to a lesser extent the fringes of the Alfama and Graça districts east of the heart of the city. LGBTQ bars and clubs cluster around the Rato, on the fringes of the Bairro Alto.

DOCKS CLUB

thedocksclub.com

This old riverfront warehouse throbs to dance music with an African beat, making it popular with the Angolan community. Tuesday is "ladies' night".
➕ Off map E9 ✉ Rua da Cintura ☎ 965 882 581 🕐 Tue, Fri, Sat–Thu 11pm–7am 🚉 Alcântara Mar (Cascais line from Cais do Sodré) 🚌 727; tram 28E

HOT CLUBE JAZZ

hcp.pt

Probably Lisbon's best venue for jazz, with Portuguese and visiting performers.
➕ J6 ✉ Praça de Alegria 48, off Avenida da Liberdade ☎ 213 460 305 🕐 Check website for concerts and sessions; Wed–Sat 10pm–2am 🚉 Avenida

KREMLIN

This is hip and difficult to get into, so dress to impress. Gets going after 2am and closes about 7am.
➕ G9 ✉ Rua Escadinhas da Praia 5 ☎ 213 957 101 🕐 Wed–Sat midnight–dawn 🚉 Santos (Cascais line from Cais do Sodré) 🚌 28, 727; tram 15, 18

O SENHOR VINHO

srvinho.com

In Lapa, this celebrated club is west of the tourist haunts of the Alfama and Bairro Alto. As a result it is more authentic—though not necessarily much cheaper—than other clubs.
➕ F8 ✉ Rua do Meio à Lapa 18 ☎ 213 972 681 🕐 Mon–Sat 7.30pm–2am 🚌 773; tram 25, 28

PAVILHÃO CHINÊS

Filled with a jumble of fans, china, sheet music and other miscellaneous *objets d'art*, this place sells reasonably priced drinks and cocktails.

➕ H7 ✉ Rua Dom Pedro V 89 ☎ 213 424 729 🕐 Mon– Sat 6pm–2am; Sun 9pm–2am 🚉 Restauradores 🚌 758

PLATEAU

If you want something a little less trendy and with more mainstream rock and pop, this is the place.
➕ G9 ✉ Rua Escadinhas da Praia 7 ☎ 213 965 116 🕐 Wed–Sat 🚉 Santos (Cascais line) from Cais do Sodré 🚌 28, 727; tram 15, 18

SOLAR DO VINHO DO PORTO

ivdp.pt

Feeling more like a private club than a bar, the port wine institute offers respite from the bustle of the Bairro Alto. Choose from an extensive list of port wines that can be tasted by the glass.
➕ J7 ✉ Rua de São Pedro de Alcântara 45 ☎ 213 475 707 🕐 Mon–Sat 11am–midnight 🚉 Baixa-Chiado, Restauradores

TRUMPS

trumps.pt

Lisbon's most popular gay club has two separate dance areas playing different sorts of music.
➕ G6 ✉ Rua da Imprensa Nacional 104b ☎ 915 938 266 🕐 Fri–Sat 11.45pm–6am (hours can be erratic) 🚉 Rato 🚌 758

COVER CHARGE

Fado houses don't charge admission, but nearly all make a cover charge. This usually buys you a couple of drinks. Performances start around 9pm, but the real action may begin only between 11pm and midnight. In theory, in most top Lisbon clubs there is no official charge at the door but drinks carry a surcharge once inside. In practice, women are rarely asked to pay at the door while the fate of their male companions depends on the mood of the doorman.

Where to Eat

PRICES

Prices are approximate, based on a 3-course meal for one person.

€€€ over €30
€€ €15–€30
€ under €15

1° DE MAIO (€€)

Traditional, good-value Portuguese cooking features here. Favorite dishes are cooked and served correctly with no concessions to foreign tastes.

➕ J7 ✉ Rua da Atalaia 8 ☎ 213 426 840 🕐 Mon–Fri 12–7; Sat 12–3 🚇 Restauradores–Elevador da Glória or Baixa-Chiado

ALFAIA (€)

restaurantealfaia.com

This restaurant, in a typical Bairro Alto establishment, is one of Lisbon's oldest. It is popular and busy at lunchtime, when seasonal specialties are served in large portions. Prices are very reasonable.

➕ J7 ✉ Travessa da Queimada 22 ☎ 213 461 232 🕐 Mon–Sat lunch, dinner; Sun dinner only 🚇 Baixa-Chiado 🚌 758, 790, 202; tram 28

COLONIAL INFLUENCE

As the Portuguese returned from the country's colonies they brought with them such dishes as *moamba* from Angola, *cachupa* from Caboverde, and tiger prawns grilled in *piri-piri* sauce from Mozambique. From Goa came the *chamuças* and curries and from Brazil the roast meats of the *picanha* and the famous bean feast known as *feijoada brasileira*. All these and many more can now be found around the city, both in their own typical restaurants and dotted through the menus of traditional Portuguese establishments.

ALI-À-PAPA (€€)

If you fancy an alternattive to solid Portuguese cooking, try this Moroccan restaurant. The evocative draperies and candles provide an authentic setting for the aromatic cuisine that focuses on quality ingredients.

➕ J7 ✉ Rua da Atalaia 95 ☎ 213 474 143 🕐 Wed–Mon dinner only 🚌 758; tram 28

BOTA ALTA (€€)

Attractive and rustic, this eaterie in the Bairro Alto serves big portions of traditional dishes that draws in the crowds.

➕ J7 ✉ Travessa da Queimada 35–37 ☎ 213 427 959 🕐 Mon–Fri lunch, dinner; Sat lunch only 🚇 Restauradores–Elevador da Glória or Baixa-Chiado 🚌 758; tram 28

CASA DA COMIDA (€€€)

casadacomida.pt

One of Lisbon's finest French-Portuguese restaurants, this is a good place to treat yourself, though it is well northwest of the city center. The setting—a former mansion in a little square—is wonderful. In summer you can eat outside.

➕ G6 ✉ Travessa das Amoireiras 1, off Rua Alexandre Herculano ☎ 213 860 889 🕐 Tue–Fri lunch, dinner; Sat–Mon dinner only 🚇 Rato 🚌 74, 711, 723

CASA FAZ FRIO (€€)

On the northern edge of the Bairro Alto, this traditional restaurant is known for its low prices and excellent seafood.

➕ H7 ✉ Rua Dom Pedro V 96 ☎ 213 461 860 🕐 Mon–Sat lunch, dinner 🚇 Restauradores–Elevador da Glória 🚌 758

COMIDA DE SANTO (€€–€€€)

comidadesanto.pt

This lively Brazilian restaurant is known for its powerful cocktails and South

American-influenced Portuguese dishes. Try the delicious *feijoada* (bean stew).

🚩 H6 ✉ Calçada Engenheiro Miguel Pais 39, off Rua da Escola Politécnica ☎ 213 963 339 🌐 Wed–Mon lunch, dinner 🚇 Rato 🚌 202, 730, 758

CONFRARIA AT YORK HOUSE (€€€)

yorkhouselisboa.com

Tucked away in a 17th-century former Carmelite convent, this restaurant, with its oasis-like courtyard, has transformed its cuisine over the last few years. An extensive selection of traditional pre-dominently Portuguese dishes are served with refined elegance.

🚩 F9 ✉ Rua das Janelas Verdes 32 ☎ 213 962 435 🌐 Wed–Sun lunch, dinner 🚌 60, 727; tram 25

ENOTECA CHAFARIZ DO VINHO (€€)

chafarizdovinho.com

In the beautiful 18th-century building known as the Chafariz do Vinho, this is an excellent place for a tapas-style plate of ham, spicy sausage and cheeses from all over Portugal, washed down with a glass of wine.

🚩 H6 ✉ Rua da Mâe d'Água ☎ 213 422 079 🌐 Tue–Sun dinner from 6pm 🚇 Restauradores–Elevador da Glória 🚌 758

ESPAÇO LISBOA (€€–€€€)

espacolisboa.pt

It is worth eating here just for the architecture. In an old factory, this huge restaurant is decorated with thousands of beautiful tiles. The menu focuses on Portuguese cooking.

🚩 Off map ✉ Rua da Cozinha Económica 16 ☎ 213 610 212 🌐 Daily lunch, dinner 🚉 Alcântara (Cascais line) from Cais do Sodré 🚌 738; tram 15, 18

FIDALGO (€€)

restaurantefidalgo.com

This popular rendezvous for media types is trendier than most Bairro Alto restaurants. The menu offers great fish dishes.

🚩 J7 ✉ Rua da Barroca 27 ☎ 213 422 900 🌐 Mon–Sat lunch, dinner 🚇 Baixa-Chiado 🚌 758; tram 28

PAP'AÇORDA (€€€)

A trendy, predominantly young, gay, arty clientele frequents this restaurant in a converted bakery. Try the *açorda* (bread soup). They have another very classy outlet in the Mercado da Ribeiro that has more space, streamlined design and a wonderful selection of changing seasonal dishes.

🚩 J7 ✉ Rua da Atalaia 57–59 ☎ 213 464 811 🌐 Tue–Sat lunch, dinner; closed first 2 weeks Jul and Nov 🚇 Baixa-Chiado 🚌 758; tram 28

PASTELARIA-PADARIA SÃO ROQUE (€)

This wonderful old bakery offers good coffee and fabulous pastries and cakes—try the *bolos de arroz* (rice flour cakes), *sonhos* (a "dream" but really a

---

BASICS

Hors d'oeuvres are *acepipes*. Breakfast is *pequeno almoço*, lunch *almoço* and dinner *jantar*. Soups are typically inexpensive and filling as a first course. Meat (*carne*) and poultry (*aves*) are usually simply grilled or fried: Roast or barbecued chicken is a particularly tasty Portuguese dish. Fish (*peixe*) and seafood (*mariscos*), though, are preeminent in Lisbon, and salt cod (*bacalhau*) and sardines (*sardinhas*) are virtually the national dishes. Vegetables are *legumes* and salad *salada*. Bread is *pão*.

doughnut) or the classic *pastel de nata* (custard tart).

🔲 J7 ⊠ Rua Dom Pedro V45 ☎ 213 224 356 🕙 Mon–Sat 7–7 🚇 Baixa-Chiado 🚌 758

PICANHA (€€)

Excellent Brazilian grilled meats, *farofa* (manioc), *feijão* (beans) and other delights are served here. Try the *caipirinhas*, alcoholic lemon punches.

🔲 F9 ⊠ Rua das Janelas Verdes 96 ☎ 213 975 401 🕙 Mon–Fri lunch, dinner; Sat, Sun dinner only 🚌 727; tram 25

PORTUGÁLIA (€€)

portugalia.pt

One of several Portugália *cervejarias* around the city, this one enjoys the best location. It sells a limited selection of good, fast food; open until late.

🔲 H9 ⊠ Doca de Santos, Cintura do Porto de Lisboa, Armazem 63 ☎ 213 422 138 🕙 Daily lunch, dinner 🚇 Cais do Sodré 🚌 All services to Cais do Sodré

PRIMAVERA (€)

This tiny restaurant (reservations are recommended) is a bastion of honest Portuguese cooking.

🔲 J8 ⊠ Travessa da Espera 34 ☎ 213 420 477 🕙 Tue–Sat lunch, dinner, Mon dinner only 🚇 Baixa-Chiado 🚌 758, 790; tram 28

RIBADOURO (€–€€)

cervejariaribadouro.pt

Eat informally at the bar or downstairs in the main restaurant. Great seafood is a specialty here, with shrimp, crayfish, lobster and crab on offer. You'll also find cod cooked in various ways.

🔲 H6 ⊠ Corner of Rua do Salitre and Avenida da Liberdade 155 ☎ 213 549 411 🕙 Daily lunch, dinner 🚇 Avenida 🚌 All services to Avenida da Liberdade

SOLAR DOS NUNES (€€)

solardosnunes.com

This small restaurant in Alcântara serves game, including wild boar, partridge and hare in season. Alternatively, try the excellent-value steaks.

🔲 Off map ⊠ Rua dos Lusíadas 70 ☎ 213 647 359 🕙 Mon–Sat lunch, dinner; closed 2 weeks Aug 🚌 738; tram 15, 18

ÚLTIMO TANGO (€–€€)

In the Bairro Alto, this Argentinian restaurant serves excellent steaks and a fine selection of Argentinian wines.

🔲 J7 ⊠ Rua Diário de Noticias 62 ☎ 213 420 341 🕙 Mon–Sat dinner only 🚌 758, 790; tram 28

XL (€€€)

The ocher-painted walls, rustic furniture and antique curiosities give this popular restaurant a homey feel. Camembert—fried in breadcrumbs and served with raspberry sauce—and soufflés are their forte.

🔲 F7 ⊠ Calçada da Estrela 57 ☎ 213 956 118 🕙 Daily dinner only 🚌 6, 13, 706, 727, 773; tram 25, 28

PORT

Port is a Douro region wine that is sweet because brandy has been added at a certain point to stop the grape sugar turning into alcohol. It may be red or white. Young red port, or *tinto*, is the most common, and is distinctive and very fruity. Reds are used to make blended ports, comprising ports from different years, the quality depending on the wines used. Reds are also the basis of vintage, ruby and tawny ports (▷ 33). White port, or *branco*, is sometimes fermented again to remove the sweetness. If chilled, this dry white port makes a delicious aperitif.

São Sebastião

Northwest of Avenida da Liberdade, stretching to the huge expanse of the Monsanto Forest park, the district of São Sebastião encompasses some of the city's major attractions and green spaces.

Top 25

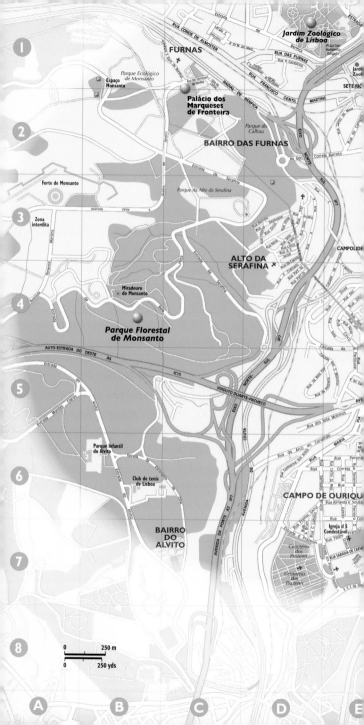

Museu Calouste Gulbenkian

- Rembrandt paintings
- Islamic ceramics
- Lalique jewelry and glass
- Carpets
- French ivory diptychs

TIPS

- Leave time to enjoy the gardens.
- Make use of the touch-screen computers.
- You can also explore the modern collection, almost next door (▷ 80).

The Museu Calouste Gulbenkian, housed in a sleek building in beautiful grounds, is one of the world's great art collections, a selection of the best of painting, furniture, ceramics, silver and decorative arts from every century, from all over the world.

Bequest to the nation The Gulbenkian is Portugal's greatest museum. Run by the Fundação Calouste Gulbenkian, it is one of the countless artistic and cultural initiatives financed by a bequest from Calouste Gulbenkian (1869–1955), an Armenian oil magnate. It was designed and built between 1964 and 1969 by architects Alberto Passoal, Pedro Cid and Ruy Jervis d'Athouguia. Gulbenkian's extensive private art collection makes up the bulk of the museum's collection, which is divided into

Clockwise from far left: portrait of Helena Fourment (c1630–32) by Rubens; stunning display of 14th-century mosque lamps; superb peacock inlaid with opals and diamonds by René Lalique; picture gallery; head of Alexander the Great; exterior of the museum

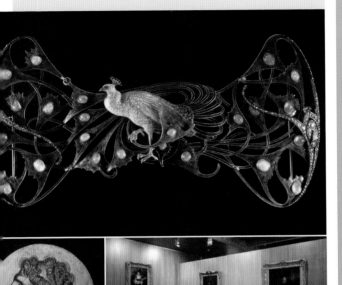

two sections: The first deals with ancient and oriental exhibits, the second with European art and objects.

Stunning collection The European section embraces paintings, sculptures and decorative arts. Exhibits are arranged chronologically and, where possible, according to school and nationality. Paintings include works by Manet, Degas, Renoir, Van Dyck, Frans Hals, Gainsborough and Turner. Pride of place goes to Rembrandt's *Alexander the Great* and *Portrait of an Old Man*. Among the tapestries, furniture, silverware and other objects, look out for the jewelry by René Lalique (in a darkened room at the end of the gallery). In the ancient and oriental sections highlights include Chinese porcelain, Japanese lacquerwork and silk and wool carpets.

THE BASICS

gulbenkian.pt

⊕ G2

✉ Avenida de Berna 45A

☎ 217 823 461

🕐 Wed–Mon 10–6. Closed public hols

🍴 Café

Ⓜ São Sebastião/Praça de Espanha

🚌 713, 716, 726, 742, 756

♿ Excellent

💲 Moderate; free on Sun

❓ Downhill from São Sebastião metro, turn right after 300m (330 yards)

Palácio dos Marqueses de Fronteira

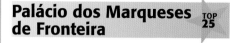

HIGHLIGHTS

- Battle Room
- Delft, or Dining, Room
- Gallery of Arts (tiled terrace)
- Chapel
- Gardens
- Doze de Inglaterra
- Statues of the Nine Muses
- Statues of Portugal's first 15 kings

TIP

- The gardens are not included in a tour when it is raining.

Not far from the city center, the beautiful Italianate gardens, stunning azulejos and grandiose interior of the Palácio dos Marqueses de Fronteira give a wonderful insight into 17th-century aristocratic taste and wealth.

Isolated beauty A metro or taxi from the Rossio drops you close to the Fronteira Palace. The palace and its gardens, an oasis of beauty in a wasteland, were founded in 1670 as a hunting lodge by João Mascarenhas, the first Marquês de Fronteira. The palace is still privately owned, but guided tours take you around some half-dozen rooms, including the Battle Room, whose tiled decoration depicts scenes from the War of Restoration. This campaign brought to an end 60 years of Spanish

Clockwise from left: the formal gardens, laid out in the 17th century; detail of azulejos (tiles) and niched statues on the exterior of the palace; part of the panels of the gallant horsemen of the Doze de Inglaterra; detail of the Doze de Inglaterra

domination of Portugal between 1581 and 1640. Fronteira was a general, and played a prominent part in the war.

Gardens The palace's Italianate gardens, full of fountains, topiary terraces and little lakes, are a delight, not least because of the *azulejos*, or tiles, which decorate virtually every suitable surface. You will already have seen a wide variety of tiles in the palace, including some of the first Delft tiles imported into Portugal (in the 17th century). In the gardens, there are benches, walls and ornamental pools swathed with tiles depicting all manner of subjects. The most eye-catching are the life-size depictions of the Doze de Inglaterra, 12 gallant horsemen who, according to legend, sailed to England to fight for the glory of rescuing 12 damsels in distress.

THE BASICS

➕ C2

✉ Largo de São Domingos de Benfica 1

☎ 217 782 023

🕐 Garden: Mon–Fri 9.30–1, 2–5, Sat 11–1. Palace: Mon–Sat guided tours at 11 and 12

🚇 Sete Rios but best visited by taxi

🚌 70

♿ Poor

💰 Gardens: moderate. Palace and gardens: expensive

❓ Tours must be booked in advance

Centro de Arte Moderna

The Centro de Arte Moderna and its outdoor sculpture exhibits are set in parkland

THE BASICS

gulbenkian.pt

➕ G2

✉ Rua Dr. Nicolau de Bettencourt

☎ 217 823 474

🕐 Wed–Mon 10–6

🍴 Café

🚇 São Sebastião/Praça de Espanha

🚌 713, 716, 726, 742, 746, 752

♿ Good

🎟 Moderate or joint ticket with Gulbenkian Museum (expensive). Free on Sun

HIGHLIGHTS

● Henry Moore
● Amadeu de Souza-Cardoso
● Guilherme Santa Rita
● Paula Rego
● Vieira da Silva
● Julio Pomar
● Costa Pinheiro

This airy museum, surrounded by gardens, gives an opportunity to trace the development of modern Portuguese art and also showcases some of the biggest 20th-century British names.

Parkland gem Lisbon's Center for Modern Art lies just around the corner from the better-known Museu Calouste Gulbenkian (▷ 76–77). Like its near neighbor, it was made possible by the legacy of Calouste Gulbenkian, the Armenian oil magnate, who left his art collection and a slice of his fortune to Portugal. The gallery is set in the same park and occupies a beautiful modern structure designed by the British architect Sir Leslie Martin. It opened in 1983. The museum's airy exhibition space—all clean lines and abundant greenery—is a pleasure in itself, admirably complementing a collection of more than 10,000 works of art.

National collection The parkland surrounding the museum is scattered with sculptures, the most notable being the *Reclining Woman* by Henry Moore, near the main entrance. Inside, the gallery's eminent Portuguese painters include Amadeu de Souza-Cardoso and Guilherme de Santa Rita, both of whom were influenced by the Italian Futurists. In acknowledging the work of foreign painters, the pair were typical of Portuguese artists, most of whom worked or studied abroad. This trend explains why few artists from Portugal are said to have strongly influenced the evolution of modern art.

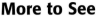

More to See

JARDIM ZOOLÓGICO DE LISBOA

zoo.pt

Lisbon's zoo stands in the former Parque das Laranjeiras, an old estate whose rose gardens, ponds and formal flower beds have been carefully preserved among the animal enclosures. The upper, northern part of the park is wilder and less cultivated, with places for picnics and leisurely exploration. In particular the Miradouro dos Moinhos (the Mill Belvedere) and the cable car both provide a broad panorama across parkland and the rest of the city. The park also has an eccentric little cemetery for dogs.

🔳 D1 ✉ Praça Marechal Humberto Delgado, Sete Rios ☎ 217 232 900 🕐 Apr–Sep daily 10–8; Oct–Mar daily 10–6 🍴 Café 🔲 Jardim Zoológico 🚍 701, 716, 726, 746, 758, 768, 770 💲 Expensive

PARQUE EDUARDO VII

At the northern end of Avenida da Liberdade, the park is laid out around two broad, mosaic-paved boulevards, which in turn are intersected by tiny walkways and carefully manicured little hedge-rows. There are panoramic views from Rua Alameda Cardeal Cerejeira on the northern side, while the wonderful cool and hot houses are lovely places to spend a tranquil half hour away from the city hustle and bustle.

🔳 G4 ✉ Praça Marquês de Pombal 🍴 Café 🔲 Parque, Marquês de Pombal 🚍 2, 12, 22, 720 and all other services to Praça Marquês de Pombal

PARQUE FLORESTAL DE MONSANTO

This enormous area of parkland on the western fringes of Lisbon is probably the city's most positive legacy of Dr. António de Oliveira Salazar (▷ 125). It is thronged on summer weekends. Take a horse and trap ride to the Miradouro de Monsanto and Miradouro dos Montes Claros

🔳 A1–C8 ✉ West of Avenida de Ceuta 🚍 723, 729, 760

Perfect tranquility in the Jardim Zoológico de Lisboa

Belém

A western suburb beside the Tejo and once a prime anchorage from where overseas expeditions set sail, Belém today is defined by its fascinating museums, monuments and spacious promenades.

Top 25

RESTELO

Rua Ricardo Rebelo

Rua A Esteves

Rua Gonçalo Velho Cabral

Rua Gonçalo Nunes

Rua Diogo de Teive

Rua Gonçalo Sintra

Museu Nac
de Etnologia

AVENIDA DAS DESCOBERTAS

Rua Antonio de Saldanha

Rua Pero de Alenquer

Rua Pero de Covilhã

Ermida
San Jerónimo

Rua Gil Eanes

Rua de Alcolena

Praça
de Goa

AVENIDA DO RESTELO

Jardim Ducla
Sorres

Praça
de Malaca

Pacheco Pereira

Rua Dom Francisco

Praça
d Damão

Praça
de Diu

Rua Dom Lourenço de Almeida

Planetário
Calouste
Gulbenkian

Rua Duarte

Rua São Francisco

de Almeida

BELÉM

Rua Tristão da Cunha

de Xavier

Rua Dom Cristóvão da Gama

R Ant d'Abreu

Vila Correia

Rua J Bastos

Museu d
Marinha

AVENIDA DA TORRE DE BELÉM

Rua de Pedrouços

Rua Bartolomeu Dias

Centro
Cultural
de Belém

Rua da Praia de Pedrouços

Rua Fernão Mendes Pinto

Rua da
Praia do
Sucesso

Centro de Arqueologia
de Lisboa

Museu
Coleção
Berardo

Univ
Moderna

ÍNDIA

AVENIDA DA

AVENIDA DE BRASÍLIA

Doca do
Bom Sucesso

Museu de
Arte Popular

Forte do
Bom Sucesso

Torre
de Belém

0   250 m
0   250 yds

a

b

1

2

3

4

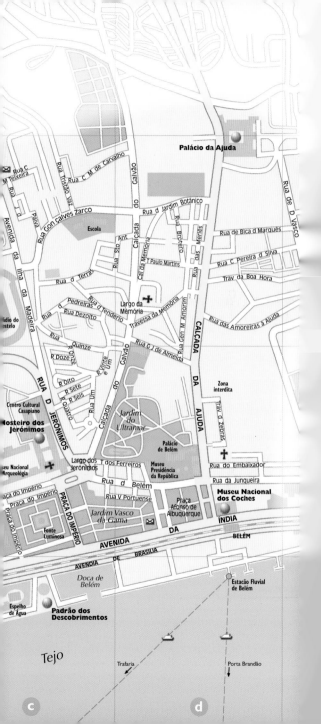

Mosteiro dos Jerónimos

HIGHLIGHTS

● South door
● West door
● Fan vaulting
● Nave
● Tomb of Vasco da Gama
● Transept star vaulting
● Choir stalls

TIP

● The monastery is always besieged by tour buses. Arrive early, visit during lunch time or wait until late afternoon to escape the buses.

There are no greater buildings in Lisbon than those of the Mosteiro dos Jerónimos, a glorious monastic complex whose carved stonework and cloisters showcase the finest Gothic and Renaissance work.

Praising the explorers The present monastery is built over the site of a small chapel erected by Henry the Navigator in 1460 to provide spiritual solace to the many seafarers who embarked on voyages of discovery from Belém. The new church was begun by Manuel I in 1502 to celebrate Vasco da Gama's successful voyage to the Indies, da Gama having held a vigil in Henry's chapel prior to his 1497 expedition. Some 50 years were to elapse before the building was completed, and during this time several architects worked on the project,

Clockwise from far left: the tomb of poet Luís de Camões basks in the sun inside the monastery; detail of a stained-glass window in the monastery church of Santa Maria; intricate detail of the ornate façade of Jerónimos monastery, displaying the Manueline style of architecture; the bell tower of the monastery

hence the mixture of Gothic, Manueline and Renaissance artistic and architectural styles.

Treasures The monastery's treasures begin with the south door, whose wealth of decoration focuses on Henry the Navigator, and the contrasting west door, featuring carvings of Manuel I, his wife, Dona Maria, and the pair's respective patron saints. Inside are soaring aisles and a breathtaking array of carved stone, reaching a climax in the sweep of fan vaulting over the nave. Search out da Gama's tomb, beneath a gallery near the church's entrance, then make for the adjoining cloisters, one of Portugal's great architectural set pieces. The two-level ensemble, particularly the lower tier, is a feast of carving, the pillars and vaults embellished with a wealth of intricately sculpted stone.

THE BASICS

mosteirojeronimos.pt

✚ c3

✉ Praça do Império

☎ 213 620 034

🕐 May–Sep Tue–Sun 10–6; Oct–Apr Tue–Sun 10–5 (last entry 30 minutes earlier)

🚌 28, 714, 727, 729, 751; tram 15

🚉 Belém (Cascais line) from Cais do Sodré

♿ Poor

💶 Church: free. Cloisters: expensive; combined tickets available with other sights

❓ Tram 15 stops outside the monastery. The return stop is 150m (165 yards) east, opposite Casa dos Pastéis

Museu Coleção Berardo

HIGHLIGHTS

- Francis Bacon
- Alexander Calder
- Willem de Kooning
- Maz Ernst
- Antony Gormley
- Jeff Koons
- Henry Moore
- Ben Nicholson
- Eduardo Paolozzi

TIP

- If you're interested in modern art, make a special trip to the Berardo rather than trying to combine it with the other Belém sights.

After years of uncertainty, Portugal's finest contemporary art collection has found a permanent home in Belém, where the stark, clean lines of the Centro Cultural form the perfect backdrop for some of the 20th century's most stunning and provocative artworks.

The collector The artworks were amassed by José Berardo (1941–), a poor boy from Madeira who left home to make his fortune at the age of 19. Astute business acumen helped turn every project he was involved with into gold, earning him a huge fortune, which he has invested in an eye-popping 20th-century art collection. In 2011, it found a permanent home in Belém. There are two exhibitions, one that spans the years 1900–1960, and the other

Two installations by Portuguese artist Rigo 23, Teko Mbarate–Struggle for Life (in the foreground) and Sapukay—Cry for Help, both 2008, were assembled in Brazil with the help of several local communities; the theme of each is the transformation of weapons—a nuclear submarine and a cluster bomb—into art

1960–2010. Every year the museum also stages a number of temporary art shows.

The collections Initially helped by Francisco Capelo, Berardo bought mainly the work of European and American artists, in a wide range of media, from the 20th to early 21st centuries, with a particular emphasis on Portuguese artists. Major movements such as surrealism, Cubism, pop art, minimalist and conceptual art are represented, with works ranging from Picasso, Miró and Piet Mondrian to Lichtenstein, Andy Warhol, Jeff Koons and the Chapman brothers. These are presented chronologically, helping you to trace the development of different artistic movements. Be sure to leave time to take in the garden, where you'll find sculpture and installations.

THE BASICS

museuberardo.pt

➕ c3

✉️ Praça do Império

☎️ 212 612 878

🕐 Tue–Sun 10–7, 24, 31; Dec 10–2.30; 1 Jan 12–7. Closed 25 Dec

🚌 714, 727, 728, 729, 751; tram 15

🚊 Belém (Cascais line)

♿ Excellent

💵 Permanent collection free; charge for some temporary exhibitions

❓ Museum shop open daily 10–7

Museu Nacional dos Coches

TOP
25

A sumptuous carriage (right) at the Coach Museum (left)

HIGHLIGHTS

● Painted ceiling vaults
● Coaches of the Marquês de Frontes
● Dom João V's state coach
● Dom José I's state coach
● King Carlos I's miniature carriage
● Maria Anna's royal carriage

The frescoed halls of the former royal riding stables are home to part of the dazzling collection of ornate 17th- to 19th-century coaches, one of Lisbon's most visited sights.

Travel in style Lisbon's National Coach Museum is one of the best collections of its type in the world. For Portuguese royalty and aristocracy, coaches and carriages were not just modes of transport, but were used to proclaim the wealth and taste of their owners. As a result, many were painted, gilded and decorated to a magnificent degree, particularly those used for ceremonial occasions. The museum, founded by Queen Amélia in 1904, is today housed in a purpose-built museum, across the road from its previous home, the former riding academy and stables of the Palácio de Belém. The new displays are stunning, but also visit the stables themselves, still home to part of the collection. The palace itself is the official residence of the Portuguese president (open Sun).

Rich collection Three of the museum's most splendid coaches were built in 1716 for the Marquês de Frontes, Portugal's ambassador to Pope Clement XI and the Holy See. They are decorated with allegorical scenes representing Portuguese military and maritime triumphs. Other highlights include cabs, prams and sedans; the royal carriage of Dom José I; a miniature carriage built for King Carlos I as a child; and Maria Anna of Austria's coach.

Padrão dos Descobrimentos

Looking out to sea—the impressive Monument to the Discoveries has intricate carvings

Jutting toward the water like the prow of a great ship, its stark profile softened by sculptures of the country's heroes, the Padrão dos Descobrimentos symbolizes both Portugal's glorious past and its national pride.

Maritime pride The Monument to the Discoveries was erected in 1960 during the Salazar dictatorship. It marked the 500th anniversary of the death of Henry the Navigator, who laid the foundation of Portugal's wide-reaching empire through his energetic support for projects such as a maritime school in the Algarve. The monument has been criticized for its vaguely fascist design and obvious nationalist intent, but it is nonetheless an architectural triumph, imposing itself on the Belém waterfront. Its jutting triangular pediment represents the prow of a ship, while the trio of curving forms above represent billowing sails. Rising over these is a redoubtable blockhouse tower, reaching some 52m (170ft) above the quayside.

Figures A procession of Portugal's great and good is carved into the pediment's sloping prow. Behind Henry, who holds a ship in his hands, stands Manuel I, who reigned from 1495 to 1521, during the height of Portugal's voyages of discovery. He is shown holding an armillary sphere, one of his regal symbols. Others include Luís de Camões, one of Portugal's most famous poets, depicted holding verses. An elevator runs to the top.

THE BASICS

padraodosdescobri
mentos.pt
⊞ c4
✉ Avenida de Brasília
☎ 213 031 950
🕐 Mar Tue–Sun 10–7;
Apr–Sep daily 10–7; Oct–
Feb Mon–Sat 10–6.
Closed public hols
🚌 28, 714, 727, 729, 751;
tram 15
🚆 Belém (Cascais line)
from Cais do Sodré
♿ Good
💰 Moderate, free Sun
until 2pm

HIGHLIGHTS

● Henry the Navigator
● Views from balcony
● Mosaic map

BELÉM TOP 25

Torre de Belém

TIPS

● The stairs up the Torre are steep and narrow and you may have to wait for access.
● To avoid the coach parties, arrive when it first opens.

Few buildings are as charming or as evocative as the Torre de Belém, a capricious confection of towers, turrets and battlements, whose ramparts are washed by the River Tejo on three sides.

National landmark Lisbon's Belém tower is not only a superb masterpiece of Renaissance and Manueline architecture, but also one of Portugal's most potent national symbols. A monument to the country's maritime triumphs across the centuries, it was built between 1515 and 1520 by Francisco de Arruda, a Portuguese architect who had worked on a variety of military projects in Morocco. His travels in North Africa made a lasting impression on him, and this is reflected in the use of Moorish motifs on the tower. Chief of these are the little domes

The tower's projecting bastion (left); a stone balcony on the elevation of the tower (middle); looking like the ultimate fairy-tale castle, the tower was built to defend Lisbon's port and was the place to keep a wary eye out for pirates coming up the River Tejo (right)

crowning the battlements, and the jutting corner sentry boxes, which are combined with arcaded windows and delicate Venetian-style loggias.

Changing roles Once the tower stood proudly out in the river, acting as a defensive bastion guarding the Restelo, or port, from pirates. Today the Tejo's ever-changing course has left it stranded on the shore. Up close, you can make out the cross motif adorning every battlement. This was the symbol of the Order of Christ, the successor to the Knights Templar in Portugal. A jutting bastion leads to a small internal cloister, below which are storerooms and dungeons. The second-level terrace—with good views—features an intricately carved statue of the Madonna (Our Lady of the Safe Homecoming). Steps lead up to the top of the tower for more views.

THE BASICS

torrebelem.pt

➕ b4

✉ Avenida de Brasília

☎ 213 620 034

🕐 May–Sep Tue–Sun 10–6.30; Oct–Apr Tue–Sun 10–5.30. Closed Mon and public hols

🚌 28, 714, 727, 729, 751; tram 15

🚉 Belém (Cascais line) from Cais do Sodré

♿ Poor

💰 Expensive; free Sun until 2pm

More to See

CENTRO CULTURAL DE BELÉM
ccb.pt

You can easily while away a few hours at this dynamic public art and performance space, known as the CCB. The hugh, stark block, with sweeping clean lines and terraces overlooking the water, was built in 1992 and is the creation of Vittorio Gregotti and Manuel Salgado.

🔢 c3 ⊠ Praça do Império ☎ 213 612 400 🕐 Mon–Fri 8–8, Sat–Sun 10–7; evening performances vary 🍴 Café 🚊 Belém 🚌 28, 714, 727, 729, 751; tram 15 💲 Free; charge for exhibitions and performances

MUSEU DE MARINHA
ccm.marinha.pt

Lisbon's maritime past is evoked in this museum, which spans the history of Portugal's seafarers from the great Age of Discoveries to the 20th century. The early explorers set out from Belém, and there are models of their boats, a wealth of artifacts and sea-going ephemera.

🔢 c3 ⊠ Praça do Império ☎ 213 620 019 🕐 Apr–Sep Tue–Sun 10–6; Oct–Mar Tue–Sun 10–5 🚊 Belém 🚌 28, 714, 727, 729, 751; tram 15 💲 Moderate; free Sun until 1pm

PALÁCIO DA AJUDA
palacioajuda.pt

Up the hill from waterside Belém is the huge neoclassical façade of the Palácio da Ajuda. Originally a low-key summer residence for the royal family, the present building dates from the early 19th century, though construction was interrupted between 1807 and 1822, when the royal family fled to Brazil to escape Napoleon. On their return, work continued spasmodically. The palace had its heyday in the 1860s, when Dom Luís I and Dona Maria were on the throne, and it's the Queen's taste behind the over-the-top decor you see today. Vast, opulent rooms, shimmering with chandeliers and glittering with gilding, come one after another, the best being the Throne Room, the banqueting hall and the ballroom. Don't miss the Queen's bedroom, with its vast chandelier, frescoed ceiling and polar-bear skin rug.

🔢 d2 ⊠ Largo da Ajuda ☎ 213 620 624 🕐 Thu–Tue 10–6. 🚊 Belém 🚌 289 from Belém; tram 18 💲 Moderate

PLANETÁRIO CALOUSTE GULBENKIAN
ccm.marinha.pt

Sponsored by the Gulbenkian Foundation, the Planetarium is in an annex of the Museu de Marinha. It hosts special children's shows.

🔢 c3 ⊠ Praça do Império ☎ 213 620 002 🕐 Shows: Wed–Thu 4pm, Sat–Sun 11 and 3.30 🚊 Belém 🚌 28, 714, 727, 729, 751; tram 15 💲 Moderate

Reach for the stars at the Planetarium

Where to Eat

PRICES	
Prices are approximate, based on a 3-course meal for one person.	
€€€	over €30
€€	€15–€30
€	under €15

ANTIGA CASA DOS PASTÉIS DE BELÉM (€)

pasteisdebelem.pt

This beautiful, blue-tiled café has been dishing up the best *pastéis de nata* (custard tarts) in Portugal since 1837, and the recipe for these tiny, flaky tarts, filled with rich vanilla custard and sprinkled with cinnamon, is a closely-guarded secret.

🔳 d1 ✉ Rua de Belém 84–92 ☎ 213 637 423 🕐 Jul–Sep daily 8–midnight; Oct–Jun daily 8–11pm 🚌 28, 727, 729, 751; tram 15

CAIS DE BELÉM (€€)

An outside terrace makes excellent use of an esplanade overlooking the park. You can expect good platefuls of Portuguese regional cooking.

🔳 d3 ✉ Rua Vieira Portuense 64 ☎ 213 621 537 🕐 Thu–Tue lunch, dinner 🚌 28, 727, 729, 751; tram 15

MERCADO DO PEIXE (€€€)

This is one of Lisbon's more upmarket fish and seafood restaurants, and it is well worth the trip out to Ajuda (just before Belém) to sample some of the best seafood the city has to offer.

🔳 d1 ✉ Estrada Pedro Teixeira ☎ 213 616 070 🕐 Tue–Sat lunch, dinner, Sun lunch only 🚌 727, 729; tram 18

O CARVOEIRO (€€)

Overlooking the park, this unpretentious restaurant attracts tourists and locals alike to sample simple meat and fish dishes that are cooked to perfection. The sardines are excellent and the portions are huge.

🔳 d3 ✉ Rua Vieira Portuense 66–68 ☎ 213 637 998 🕐 Tue–Sat lunch, dinner, Sun lunch only 🚌 28, 727, 729, 751; tram 15

O CASEIRO (€€–€€€)

Locals flock to this simple Portuguese restaurant, which serves generous portions of good, uncomplicated food. There are vaulted ceilings and walls hung with air-cured hams and pumpkins.

🔳 d3 ✉ Rua de Belém 35 ☎ 213 638 803 🕐 Mon–Sat lunch, dinner; closed Aug 🚌 28, 727, 729, 751; tram 15

PORTUGALIA (€€)

portugalia.pt

Enjoy a great view of the Padrão at this peaceful eating house, set on a little island on an artificial lake. The menu includes *bitoques* (steak) and delicious *gambas* (prawns).

🔳 c4 ✉ Avenida de Brasília, Edif. Esplho d'Agua ☎ 213 032 700 🕐 Daily noon–midnight 🚌 28, 727, 729, 751; tram 15

CHARGES AND TIPS
Restaurants will often bring plates of starters such as bread, ham, cheese, and olives. These will be charged to your bill as *couvert*, or cover charge, unless you send them back. Very few people do this as they are great and unless you are in a very fancy restaurant they will make little difference to the final bill. Value-added tax, or IVA, is added to restaurant bills at 8 per-cent. Most bills say *IVA incluido,* so already include this charge. Tips are welcomed and generally expected as a service charge is rarely included on the bill. Anything from 5 percent is considered acceptable.

Farther Afield

Just a few bus or metro stops away and you are in the city's suburbs, where you'll discover a plethora of other attractions to keep you busy for a long time.

Museu Nacional do Azulejo

HIGHLIGHTS

● Tiled Manueline cloisters
● Lisbon cityscape (1738)
● Tiled nativity (1580)
● Tiled battle scenes
● The Hunting Room, with a distinctive Far Eastern theme
● Igreja da Madre de Deus—stunning tiling, carving, gilding and fresco in an architecturally superb church

This lovely museum, which includes the tranquil Igreja da Madre de Deus church, traces the history of tile-making. Through Dutch, Moorish and Hispanic influences, here you'll see the Portuguese emerge as masters of their craft.

Simple and sophisticated The museum's earliest *azulejos* (a corruption of the Arabic word *azraq*—azure—or *zalayja*, meaning a smooth stone or polished terracotta) date from the beginning of the 16th century. Later exhibits show how simple, single-hued designs gave way to more sophisticated patterning allowed by new majolica techniques imported from Italy. As the art developed, *azulejos* became still more complex and vibrant. Later still, they were influenced by the single-motif

Behind the gates (left), the Museu Nacional do Azulejo conceals superb tiled artworks, such as this panorama of Lisbon's waterfront from 1738 (right); the whole piece is 36m (120ft) long

patterns of Dutch tiles and by the fashion for blue and white inspired by the arrival of Ming dynasty porcelain in Europe. Simpler designs also resulted from the 1755 earthquake, when large numbers of cheap decorative tiles were required for rebuilding the city.

Museum highlights The museum is full of beautiful examples. Look for the 36m (120ft) tiled cityscape of Lisbon, made in 1738, prior to the 1755 earthquake, and the small Manueline cloister decorated with its original 16th- and 17th-century tiles. Also, don't miss the fine, 16th-century polychrome tile picture of Nossa Senhora da Vida, a nativity scene. There are delightful 18th-century blue-and-white tile scenes of everyday life, such as a doctor giving an injection to a patient.

THE BASICS

museudoazulejo.gov.pt
⊞ See map ▷ 99
⊠ Rua da Madre de Deus 4
☎ 218 100 340
⏰ Tue–Sun 10–6
🍴 Café
🚊 Santa Apolonia, then bus 794
🚌 718, 742, 794
♿ Poor
💶 Moderate. Free on Sun and public hols until 2pm

Parque das Nações

HIGHLIGHTS

- Oceanário
- Teleférico (cable car)
- Pavilhão do Conheci-mento–Ciência Viva
- Vasco de Gama mall
- Waterside gardens

In contrast to historic Lisbon's steep hills and narrow streets, this stretch of futuristic waterfront development is where you will discover the face of the 21st-century city, set among wide promenades and waterside gardens.

Background Once a derelict industrial zone, the area was redeveloped as the high-tech site for Expo '98, opening at the same time as the neighboring 167km-long (103-mile) Vasco da Gama bridge. Today, it's one of Lisbon's prime playgrounds, thronged every weekend.

Getting started As soon as you arrive at the iconic Gare do Oriente station it is obvious you are stepping into a very different Lisbon. You pass straight into the Vasco da Gama shopping

Clockwise from far left: Torre Vasco da Gama, the Vasco da Gama observation tower; Banners and a field of bloom; the Vulcão de Água fountain near the Oceanário; Wall of Water fountain

mall—Lisbon's biggest shopping and leisure complex, occupying four floors. Pick up a plan of the Parque at the information desk. If you want transport take the miniature train around the Parque.

What to do The area contains two of Lisbon's largest concert venues, a casino, hotels and a plethora of eating and drinking options, plus major attractions such as the Oceanário (▷ 105) and the Pavilhão do Conhecimento—Ciência Viva (▷ 105). There are also play areas and bike rental. Take the cable car (Teleférico) from the waterfront for a bird's-eye view of the complete site: At the north end is the Torre Vasco da Gama (closed to visitors), built as a symbol of the great 15th-century voyager. Don't miss a stroll among the waterfront gardens.

THE BASICS

portaldasnacoes.pt
🕂 See map ▷ 99
✉ Alameda dos Oceanos
☎ 218 919 333; cable car 218 956 143; shopping mall 218 930 600
🕐 Cable car: Oct–Feb 11–6; Mar–Jun & Oct 11–7; Jul–Aug 10.30–7 Shopping mall: daily 9–midnight
🍽 Restaurants and cafés
🚇 Oriente
♿ Cable car: moderate. Prices for Oceanário and Pavilhão do Conhecimento–Ciência Viva (▷ 105). Inclusive ticket *Cartão do Parque* for all main sights: expensive

More to See

MUSEU DE LISBOA
museudelisboa.pt

The Museum of the City lies in the northwest corner of the Campo Grande. A stimulating museum in a lovely setting, it uses paintings, prints and drawings to trace the development of Lisbon. Highlights include a model of pre-earthquake Lisbon, a 17th-century painting showing the Praça do Comércio before the Marqués de Pombal renovated it, and a picture of the poet Fernando Pessoa, painted in 1954.
➕ See map ▷ 98 ✉ Campo Grande 245 ☎ 217 513 200 🕐 Tue–Sun 10–6 🚇 Campo Grande 🚌 738, 745, 750, 767 💷 Inexpensive. Free on Sun

MUSEU DA MÚSICA
museunacionaldamusica.gov.pt

A collection of musical instruments from around Europe, dating from the 16th to 21st centuries.
➕ See map ▷ 98 ✉ Rua João Freitas Branco ☎ 217 710 990 🕐 Tue–Sat 10–6 🚇 Alto dos Moinhos 🚌 768 💷 Inexpensive; under-12s free

MUSEU NACIONAL DO TEATRO E DA DANÇA
museunacionaldoteatroedanca.pt

The National Theater Museum concentrates on the personalities who have graced the Lisbon stage over the years, which makes it of limited interest to the foreign visitor. It's worth a look if you're visiting the area's Costume Museum (▷ below), as it also has theatrical costumes, props, photographs, stage designs and other ephemera.
➕ See map ▷ 98 ✉ Parque do Monteiro-Mor, Estrada do Lumiar 10 ☎ 217 567 410 🕐 Tue–Sun 10–6. Closed public hols 🚇 Lumiar 🚌 703, 796 💷 Moderate; joint ticket with Museu Nacional do Traje. Free Sun until 2pm

MUSEU NACIONAL DO TRAJE
museudotraje.gov.pt

The National Museum of Costume occupies the tiled and frescoed Palácio do Duque de Palmela, also known as the Palácio Monteiro-Mor, in the Parque do Monteiro-Mor at Lumiar. Visit the Jardim Botânico,

The National Theater Museum set in the lush Parque do Monteiro-Mor

dotted with pools, plants and trees, as well as the museum itself, which has beautiful old tapestries, jewels, toys and costumes.

🔲 See map ▷ 98 ✉ Parque do Monteiro-Mor, Largo Júlio de Castilho, Lumiar ☎ 217 567 620 🕐 Tue–Sun 10–6 (closes at 5 in winter) 🚇 Lumiar 🚌 703, 796 💷 Moderate; joint ticket with Museu Nacional do Teatro. Free Sun until 2pm

OCEANÁRIO

oceanario.pt

Spectacularly designed by Peter Chermayeff, this is one of Europe's largest oceanariums, with species from the five different oceans. The vast central tank, Global Ocean, is surrounded by four smaller tanks with two viewing levels. You'll encounter sharks, manta, barracudas, ocean sunfish, rays and giant groupers. Begin on the upper level, passing through different climatic zones—the puffins, penguins and otters are the draw here. Move down to the lower level to discover an underwater environment.

Additional smaller tanks enclose such wonders as living coral reefs, mangrove forests and Australian dragon fish—their camouflage so impressive it is almost impossible to detect them against the weeds.

🔲 See map ▷ 99 ✉ Esplanada Dom Carlos I, Doca dos Olivais, Parque das Nações ☎ 218 917 000 🕐 Apr–Oct daily 10–8; Nov–Mar daily 10–7 🚇 Oriente 💷 Expensive

PAVILHÃO DO CONHECIMENTO—CIÊNCIA VIVA

pavconhecimento.pt

This science and technology museum stimulates scientific enquiry using experimental methods and exploration. Through exhibitions and interactive activities, visitors can discover science in an enjoyable way. There is a shop where you can buy science-related gifts to follow up your day at the museum.

🔲 See map ▷ 99 ✉ Alameda dos Oceanos, Parque das Nações ☎ 218 917 100 🕐 Tue–Fri 10–6, Sat, Sun 11–7 🚇 Oriente 💷 Expensive

Some of the 7,000 or so costumes exhibited at the National Museum of Costume

Watch out! There are sharks about in the Oceanário

Excursions

MAFRA

The little town of Mafra is dominated by the monumental Palácio-Convento, one of the largest baroque monasteries and palaces in Europe. Begun in 1717, the Palácio was built by Dom João V, who had pledged to build a monastery should he and his wife have a child. Bárbara, the future Queen of Spain, was born within a year. Finance for the project was provided by the gold and diamonds of Brazil. The plan was for a monastery of 13 monks—in the end it housed 300. Around 50,000 workers and 7,000 soldiers toiled on the building. Tours include the monastery, but it's the royal apartments, grandeur on a vast scale, complete with separate suites for both king and queen, that you'll remember.

SINTRA

Sintra, an easy journey out from Lisbon and beautifully set on hillsides, is rich in splendid royal palaces and lush vegetation. The sights are not within walking distance, so you will need to use the efficient bus service, taxis or a car, or join an organized tour. In Sintra-Vila (the town itself) the main thing to see is the Palácio Nacional, begun by Dom João I in the 15th century and used as a royal palace until the end of the 19th century. Just south of Sintra-Vila lies the Castelo dos Mouros, a Moorish castle begun in the 8th century. The views from its rocky pinnacles are magnificent. Farther south, around 3km (1.8 miles) from Sintra-Vila, lies another royal palace, the Palácio da Pena, a wonderfully pretentious monument built in the 19th century. A madcap medieval pastiche, its exterior is all battlements and towers. Its park and gardens are delightful, and the views from its terraces sublime. The restored Quinta da Regaleira, just to the east of Sintra, is one of the finest examples of late 19th-century revivalist art. It has a Masonic "well of initiation", gargoyles, mythological grottos and neo-Manueline palace and chapel.

Ranging from luxurious converted palaces and modern upmarket hotels to simple *residências* and *pensões*, Lisbon has accommodations to suit everyone.

Introduction

If you like to be in the thick of things, the Baixa and Chiado areas are the places to be, but for something more peaceful and still close to the action, choose a hotel on or around Avenida da Liberdade. In the Alfama district you will find *pensões* still living in the past, while some of Lisbon's best hotels, housed in elegant historic buildings, are in the prosperous suburb of Lapa.

Getting the Best Price

Bear in mind rates vary according to season and will soar in peak periods (by as much as 40 percent). Hotels often quote their highest rates, but don't be afraid to ask if they have a less expensive room. In Portugal hotels and *pensões* are legally required to post the room rates on the back of the bedroom door, which should include IVA (VAT). If you have a child with you, most hotels will put an extra bed in the room for a small charge.

What to Expect

As in most major European cities, Portugal's hotels are graded between one and five stars, the facilities, service and comfort reflected in the price and rating. *Pensões* and *residências* are good budget options; their main distinction being that *residências* are unlikely to serve meals other than breakfast. These are classified, from one to three stars—a three-star *pensão* would cost about the same as a one-star hotel. Budget options, though scrupulously clean, often have old fashioned facilities and decor.

BOOKING AHEAD

Before you book accommodations it's worth checking out internet sites such as laterooms.com, expedia.com and lastminute.com, though you may find that your chosen hotel's own website actually offers the best value, with reductions for stays of three nights or more. If you want to be independent have a look at airb&b.com or, for a good range of self-catering apartments, homeaway.co.uk or ownersdirect.co.uk, where you'll find plenty of choice in the city center.

Budget Hotels

HOTEL BORGES

borgeschiadohotel-lisbon.com

A comfortable if unexceptional hotel, Borges is close to the Chiado shopping district. It is popular, so book ahead.

➕ J8 ✉ Rua Garrett 108–110 ☎ 210 456 400 🚇 Baixa-Chiado 🚋 Tram 28

PENSÃO LONDRES

pensaolondres.com.pt

This friendly and efficient pension in an old townhouse is plusher than most in its price category. Rooms vary considerably; some on the fourth floor have views, so look first.

➕ H7 ✉ Rua Dom Pedro V 53 ☎ 213 462 203 🚌 758, 773, 790

PENSÃO PORTUENSE

pensaoportuense.com

All rooms in this family-run guesthouse are simple, clean and spacious; no frills, but excellent value and friendly staff.

➕ J7 ✉ Rua das Portas de Santo Antão 149–157 ☎ 213 464 197 🚇 Restauradores 🚌 All services to Restauradores

PENSÃO RESIDENCIAL ROYAL

royal-guesthouse.com

Possibly one of the best deals in central Lisbon, this small *residência* in the Baixa offers clean, freshly decorated rooms with en-suite bathrooms.

➕ K8 ✉ Rua do Crucifixo 50–3° ☎ 213 479 006 🚇 Baixa-Chiado

RESIDENCIAL AVENIDA PARQUE

avenidaparque.com

A great-value *residência* overlooking the Parque Eduardo VII. A recent overhaul has transformed the public areas; bedrooms are spacious and bright and some have balconies. Some of the rooms sleep 2, 3, or 4, which is ideal for families, as is the location in this area of Lisbon, away from the crowded streets of the old town.

➕ H4 ✉ Avenida Sidónio Pais 6 ☎ 213 532 181 🚇 Parque

RESIDENCIAL CAMÕES

pensaoresidencialcamoes.com

A perfect location in the Bairro Alto is the main selling point of this friendly *residência*. It has small, attractive rooms and nice communal areas. The more expensive rooms have balconies and/or private bathrooms.

➕ J7 ✉ Travessa do Poço da Cidade 38–1° ☎ 213 467 510 🚇 Rossio, Baixa-Chiado 🚌 758

SÉ GUESTHOUSE

This welcoming guesthouse is in a pleasant and well-located town house. Bathrooms are shared, although there are two rooms with ensuite, and the light and airy rooms are smart. All have TVs. A good breakfast is included in the room rate.

➕ L8 ✉ Rua São João da Praça 97–1° ☎ 218 864 400 🚌 37; tram 12, 28

Mid-Range Hotels

Expect to pay between €100 and €250 per night for a double room in a mid-range hotel.

AS JANELAS VERDES

heritage.pt

An intimate hotel in an 18th-century town house, this has spacious and sumptuously fitted rooms. The location means the front rooms can be noisy but the romantic, "boutique" ambience more than makes up for this.

➕ F9 ✉ Rua das Janelas Verdes 47 ☎ 213 968 143 🚇 Santos (from Cais do Sodré) 🚌 727; tram 25

BRITÂNIA

heritage.pt

A traditional hotel built in 1944 , Britânia lies just east of the Avenida da Liberdade. It retains an old-fashioned charm. Expect courteous service. Breakfast is the only meal served.

➕ H5 ✉ Rua Rodrigues Sampaio 17 ☎ 213 155 016 🚇 Avenida 🚌 711, 732, 745, all services to Avenida da Liberdade

EVER LISBOA

everhotels.com

This palatial town house, built in 1886 by a wealthy lawyer, offers excellent value for money. A vibrant mural of Lisbon adorns the grand staircase that leads to 32 modest but spacious and well-equipped bedrooms.

➕ J6 ✉ Avenida da Liberdade 189 ☎ 213 522 618 🚇 Avenida 🚌 All services to Avenida da Liberdade

EXECUTIVE

executive.sanahotels.com

Small and very attractively fitted out, this modern hotel is close to the Gulbenkian, so not central but with good transport to central Lisbon. There is no restaurant but breakfast is served.

➕ H2 ✉ Avenida Conde de Valbom 56–62 ☎ 217 951 157 🚇 São Sebastião 🚌 16, 36, 726, 746

HERITAGE AV LIBERDADE

heritage.pt

The deep blue facade draws attention to this charming small boutique hotel, housed in a restored late 18th-century building in the historic heart of the city. The interior combines stylish modern design with traditional Portuguese touches.

➕ J6 ✉ Avenida da Liberdade 28 ☎ 213 404 040 🚇 Avenida 🚌 All services to Avenida da Liberdade

LISBOA REGENCY CHIADO

lisboaregencychiado.com

This boutique hotel is located right in the heart of the city's smartest shopping district, with great views of the Castelo. The bedrooms are a mix of Portuguese and oriental design and all have modern facilities. You can enjoy an excellent

WHERE TO STAY

Of the more expensive hotels, the older ones tend to be close to the Rossio, while the newer establishments are in the north on, or just off, the Avenida da Liberdade. Other choice hotels are in residential suburbs well away from the heart of the city, mostly in the west or northeast. Most budget options are near the Rossio and in the Baixa, but these central locations are likely to be noisy unless you can secure an off-street room. Two of the city's most picturesque places to stay, the atmospheric Bairro Alto and Alfama districts, have relatively few hotels.

breakfast while gazing over the rooftops through the bay windows.

➕ K8 ✉ Rua Nova do Almada 114 ☎ 213 256 100 🚇 Baixa-Chiado 🚌 758

MÉTROPOLE

almeidahotels.com

An imposing and elegant building located in the Rossio, the Métropole is central but consequently also noisy. The air-conditioning and double-glazing help.

➕ K7 ✉ Praça Dom Pedro IV 30 ☎ 213 219 030 🚇 Rossio

MIRAPARQUE

miraparque.com

This almost perfect mid-range friendly hotel lies on a quiet tree-lined street overlooking the Parque Eduardo VII and Pavilhão dos Desportos. Rooms are a little dated, but they are large, bright and spotlessly clean. It serves good Portuguese food, and is only a minute from the metro.

➕ H4 ✉ Avenida Sidónio Pais 12 ☎ 213 524 286 🚇 Parque

MUNDIAL

hotel-mundial.pt

Opened in 1958, this large hotel has been thoroughly refurbished over the years. The 373 modern bedrooms are a good size and have big picture windows. It is situated in the heart of Lisbon close to Rossio and within easy walking distance of many restaurants and attractions.

➕ K7 ✉ Praça Martim Moniz 2 ☎ 218 842 000 🚇 Rossio

SENHORA DO MONTE

albergaria-senhora-do-monte.lisbon-hotel.org

This lovely hilltop hotel in the Graça district, north of the Castelo, would definitely be the first choice in its category if

it were closer to the inner city. It has 28 attractive rooms, some with balconies and air-conditioning, and a relaxed and amiable ambience. It has no restaurant on site, but breakfast is served.

➕ L6 ✉ Calçada do Monte 39 ☎ 218 866 002 🚇 Martim Moniz 🚌 708; tram 12, 28

SOLAR DOS MOUROS

solardosmouroslisboa.com

This small unique hotel in the Alfama district is ideal for romantic art lovers. The 12 individual bedrooms—including a duplex suite—are decorated with African art and wonderful abstract pieces by owner-painter Luís Lemos. All rooms have a lovely view either over the castle or the river.

➕ L7 ✉ Rua do Milagre de Santo António 6 ☎ 218 854 940 🚌 Tram 28

YORK HOUSE

yorkhouselisboa.com

Although York House is situated to the west of the heart of the city, it is one of Lisbon's most popular hotels, thanks to its lovely tree- and plant-filled court-yard, and 34 simple but tastefully decorated rooms.

➕ F9 ✉ Rua das Janelas Verdes 32 ☎ 213 962 435 🚇 Santos 🚌 727; tram 25

NOISE

Lisbon is notoriously noisy. Expensive hotels are not immune to the cacophony, but most have double-glazing and air-conditioning, which provide a measure of protection. Cheaper hotels are usually not so blessed, and may be near the Rossio, Baixa or Bairro Alto, three of the city's busier districts. Try to avoid rooms on the street, and check for bars or restaurants nearby, which are likely to be open until the small hours.

Luxury Hotels

AVENIDA PALACE

hotelavenidapalace.pt

A traditional hotel in the heart of the city, the Avenida was built in 1842 between the busy Rossio and Praça dos Restauradores. The rooms away from the street are calm, comfortable and spacious. Be sure to check internet rates for good reductions.

➕ J7 ✉ Rua 1 de Dezembro 123 ☎ 213 218 100 🚇 Rossio

LAPA PALACE

olissipo-lapa-palace.lisbon.com

This 94-room five-star hotel in Lisbon is one of the most expensive. It divides between a 19th-century palace and a modern six-floor block with luxurious rooms. It has a lovely garden with pool.

➕ E8 ✉ Rua do Pau de Bandeira 4 ☎ 213 949 494 🚇 Santos 🚌 713; tram 25

PALACETE CHAFARIZ DEI REI

chafarizdeirei.com

This elegant, traditional and beautiful hotel dates from 1909, when it was the home of a Brazilian merchant. The decor, both inside and out, combines art nouveau with classic elegance in a building flooded with light. Almost all the huge rooms have river views.

➕ L8 ✉ Tv Chafariz dei Rei 6 ☎ 218 886 150 🚌 25

PALÁCIO DE BELMONTE

palaciobelmonte.com

This beautiful 16th-century palace in the Alfama district has been painstakingly restored to make it one of the world's finest luxury hotels. State-ofthe-art comfort combines with sheer elegance in the seven individual suites, which are decorated with 18th-century *azulejos* and have amazing views. The peaceful terraces and gardens are arranged around a black marble pool.

➕ L8 ✉ Páteo Dom Fradique 14 ☎ 218 816 600 🚌 Tram 28

PESTANA PALACE

pestana.com

This beautiful yellow 19th-century palace set in wonderful grounds may be a little way out of the city center, but it is perfect for an indulgent break relaxing by the pool in opulent surroundings. The 193 rooms and 4 suites are amazing and the restaurant is excellent.

➕ Off map ✉ Rua Jaú 54, Ajuda ☎ 213 615 600 🚌 738, 742; tram 18

RITZ FOUR SEASONS

fourseasons.com

Lisbon's most famous deluxe hotel opened in the 1950s. All of the 310 rooms have their own balconies with a view of the old town or Parque Eduardo VII. It has a pool, spa facilities and on-site car parking.

➕ G5 ✉ Rua Rodrigo do Fonseca 88 ☎ 213 811 400 🚇 Marquês de Pombal 🚌 702, 711, 713, 723

Lisbon's bus and metro service is excellent, but it is often best to get around on foot, making use of the odd tram trundling up the steep cobbled streets or the elevator to whisk you to the top of the hill.

Planning Ahead

When to Go

Lisbon's hottest and busiest months are July and August; many of the city's inhabitants take their holiday then so some shops and restaurants may be shut. The best months to visit are April, May, June, September and October, when the city is less busy and the weather is mild.

<table>
<tr><td colspan="2">TIME</td></tr>
<tr><td colspan="2">Portugal observes the same time as Britain, and is 5 hours ahead of New York and 8 hours ahead of Los Angeles.</td></tr>
</table>

AVERAGE DAILY MAXIMUM TEMPERATURES

JAN	FEB	MAR	APR	MAY	JUN	JUL	AUG	SEP	OCT	NOV	DEC
57°F	59°F	63°F	67°F	71°F	77°F	81°F	82°F	79°F	72°F	63°F	58°F
14°C	15°C	17°C	20°C	21°C	25°C	27°C	28°C	26°C	22°C	17°C	15°C

Spring (March–May): Often mild and sunny. Rainfall is often high in March but usually decreases quickly in April and May.

Summer (June–September): Hot and dry, but the heat is tempered by cooling sea breezes. Rain is rare in July and August, but there may be thunderstorms.

Autumn (October–November): Temperatures remain good, with many balmy days, and often clear skies, but rain picks up in October and November.

Winter (December–February): Lisbon bears the brunt of wet Atlantic depressions and rainfall is highest in December and January, with February a little drier.

WHAT'S ON

February/March *Carnival celebrations*: Parades, parties and fancy dress.

March *Moda Lisboa*: Lisbon's top fashion event.

March/April *Calvary Procession*: Through the Graça district on Good Friday. Easter celebrations throughout the city.

April *Carnation Revolution*: Celebrations to commemorate 25 April 1974.

Indie Lisboa: International film festival (mid-April).

May *Pilgrimage*: The first annual pilgrimage to Fátima (13 May).

May/June *Rock in Lisboa*: Running over two weekends and attracting big international bands.

June *Major feast days*: 13 June (St. Antony); 24 June (St. John); 29 June (St. Peter). *The Festas dos Santos* (Festivals of the Saints) take place on and around these three days.

Sintra Festival: Classical music and dance in Sintra's churches and palaces (June and July).

Flea Market: At Sintra (29 June).

August *International Summer Jazz Festival*: Organized by the Calouste Gulbenkian Foundation.

September *Opera Season*: Starts at the Teatro Nacional de São Carlos and runs through to June.

October *Pilgrimage*: The second annual pilgrimage to Fátima (mid-October).

EDP Rock'n' Roll Lisbon Marathon: Around 3,000 runners follow the River Tejo from Cascais to the Parque das Nações.

Lisbon Online

carris.pt

Carries full details of the tram and bus routes run by Carris, the company responsible for most public transportation in the city. Also has pages about its various city sightseeing tours.

metrolisboa.pt

An excellent site (with English section), with all you need to know about routes, tickets and more on the Lisbon metro system.

ana.pt

Portugal's official airport website, with good information on all aspects of the city's Portela Airport, plus other useful tourist information.

visitportugal.com

The official site of the Portuguese trade and tourism organization, with tourist information on the country as a whole, including Lisbon.

golisbon.com

An independent site packed with useful and sometimes quirky information; it's particularly strong on up-to-the-minute listings.

ccb.pt

The site of the Cultural Center of Belém provides information on forthcoming concerts, exhibitions and other events, as well as highlighting other aspects of the facility's work.

portaldasnacoes.pt

An all-embracing site for the attractions, events and activities at the vast Parque das Nações, the former Expo 98 site.

ipmuseus.pt

An official site that covers most of Portugal's museums, with links to individual galleries.

dn.pt

Listings in Portuguese on the website of the daily newspaper *Diario de Notícias*.

USEFUL SITES

visitlisboa.com
The official site of the Lisbon tourist office, with comprehensive details of hotels, restaurants, transport, museums and other attractions (in English).

fodors.com
A travel-planning site. You can research prices and weather, book tickets, cars and rooms, and ask fellow visitors questions. There are also links to other sites.

INTERNET AND MOBILE COVERAGE

Pronto Net
As you would expect in a capital city, mobile reception in Lisbon and the surrounding area is excellent. Most hotels offer free WiFi, though in budget options it may only be available in the reception area. You can also get connected at most large cafés, bars and restaurants.

Getting There

ENTRY REQUIREMENTS

For the latest passport and visa information, check the British embassy website at gov.uk, the United States embassy at pt.usembassy. gov or for Canadians, travel.gc.ca

TOURIST INFORMATION

● Main offices:
Lisboa Welcome Center
Praça do Comércio
☎ 910 517 886 🅲 Daily 9–8
Palácio Foz ✉ Praça dos Restauradores ☎ 213 463 314 🅲 Daily 9–8
● There are other offices or kiosks at **Santa Apolónia railway station** ☎ 910 517 982 🅲 Summer Mon–Sat 9–8; winter Wed–Sat 8–1
Bélem ✉ Mosteiro dos Jerónimos ☎ 213 658 435 🅲 Summer daily 9–7; winter Tue–Sat 10–1, 2–6
Portela Airport ☎ 218 450 660 🅲 Daily 7am–midnight

AIRPORTS

Internal and international flights use Lisbon's Portela Airport, 7km (4 miles) north of the city. The arrivals hall has a tourist information office, car-rental desks and restaurants. Left luggage is available on the ground level of the P2 parking lot (north end of arrivals hall).

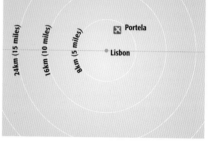

FROM PORTELA AIRPORT

For flight information consult the website (ana. pt) or call 218 413 500. The Aerobus (carris. pt) leaves from outside the arrivals hall every 20 minutes (daily 7am–11pm), making stops in and around the city. Journey time is 20–40 minutes. Tickets (from the driver) cost €4 and are also valid for a day's travel on the Carris public transport network. Regular city buses (Nos. 208, 705, 722, 744 and 783) leave from outside the airport for various areas of the city, and cost about €1.40. There is a metro connection between the airport and Saldanha station; travel time 20 minutes, cost €1.40.

Taxis operate around the clock from outside the terminal. A ride to the heart of the city should cost €15–€20 (plus €1.50 for luggage and supplements after 10pm and weekends and public holidays). Beware, airport taxis are notorious for overcharging; check that the meter is running or fix a price first, or better still, buy a prepaid taxi voucher from the tourist office in the arrivals hall. Most well-known car-rental companies have desks in the arrivals hall.

ARRIVING BY BUS

International and main regional bus services arrive at Terminal Rodoviario at Sete Rios, next to the Jardim Zoológico metro station, just north of the Sete Rios train station. The main national long-distance operator is Rede Expressos (tel 707 223 344; rede-expressos.pt), with services from Porto, Faro and other destinations, plus Seville in Spain. International bus services include a daily Eurolines service (tel 08717 818181 (UK number); eurolines.co.uk) from London via Paris. Journey time is 42 hours.

ARRIVING BY CAR

If you are driving to Lisbon, all routes run through Spain. The best and safest option is the E-4 Euro-route, which runs from Madrid via Badajoz. Once in Portugal, it becomes the A6/A2 and heads through the Alentejo to Palmela, where you can choose to continue on the A2 to reach Lisbon via the Ponte 25 de Abril to the city's west, or take the A12 and cross the Tejo on the Ponte Vasco da Gama to the east. The quickest way by car to Lisbon from the UK is by ferry to Bilbao (29–35 hours) or Santander (24 hours). The drive from Santander to Lisbon via Spain and northern Portugal is about 1,000km (620 miles).

ARRIVING BY TRAIN

International trains and services from Porto, Coimbra and other northern towns, plus northern and western suburban services, arrive at Santa Apolónia (tel 707 210 220). Alternatively you can get off at the Gare do Oriente station at the Parque das Nações and connect with the metro. Trains from the Algarve and elsewhere in the south arrive at Oriente or you can get off at Entrecampos, which is more central, and connect with the metro. Cais do Sodré has services to and from Estoril and Cascais; Rossio and Sete Rios have trains to Sintra, Mafra and other suburban and west-coast destinations. Caminhos de Ferro Portugueses is the national rail company (tel 707 208 220; cp.pt).

Getting Around

TOURIST CARD

The highly recommended Lisbon Tourist Card (lisboacard.org) gives free admittance to virtually all city museums and other attractions, and unlimited use of public transport. There is also a 65 percent discount on the Aerobus airport shuttle. It is valid for 24, 48 or 72 hours (€19/€32/€40), and is sold at many outlets, including the tourist offices listed on page 116. Children pay a reduced price. Prepaid taxi vouchers and a 72-hour Eat and Shop card (▷ 10) are also available from the tourist offices. The last provides discounts at a limited number of selected shops and restaurants.

LOST PROPERTY

Police
First port of call should be the Tourist Police (▷ panel, 121), who have an office open 24 hours.

Metro
✉ Marquês do Pombal Metro, North atrium or Terreiro do Paço ☎ 213 500 115 🕐 Mon–Fri 8.30–7.30

BUSES, TRAMS AND ELEVATORS

Most buses, trams (*eléctricos*) and elevators (*elevadores*) in Lisbon are run by Carris (tel 213 500 115; carris.pt)—yellow booths around the city provide maps, tickets and information. Buy tickets (interchangeable between buses, trams and *elevadores*) from drivers or kiosks; a pass is the best value (▷ 119). The Elevador de Santa Justa runs from Rua Áurea (Rua do Ouro) in the Baixa to Largo do Carmo in the Bairro Alto; the Elevador da Glória funicular runs from Praça dos Restauradores to Rua São Pedro de Alcântara in the Bairro Alto; and the Elevador da Bica goes from Rua de São Paulo to Largo Calhariz-Rua do Loreto. Tickets can be bought from machines (not from the driver) on the new large trams (notably the No. 15). You must have the right coins. Tickets must be validated the first time you use them in the machines on board.

DRIVING IN LISBON

Traffic jams, car theft and a lack of parking make having a car in Lisbon a headache. If you do drive, use a meter or official parking lot. Improperly parked cars are towed away—the local PSP Police station will have details of the nearest pound. Holders of old UK pre-EU green licenses should carry an International Driving Permit (IDP). US licenses are accepted.

GUIDED TOURS

Trams are an inexpensive way of seeing the city. Tram 28 runs from the Church of São Vicente in the east to the Jardim da Estrela in the west, via the Baixa. Other good routes include the No. 12 from São Tomé to Largo Martim Moniz and the Nos. 15 or 18 (not Sunday) along the waterfront from Praça do Comércio through Belém to Algés. There are two tourist tram routes available: Circuito Colinas and Circuito Descobrimentos; and six open-top bus routes including the Circuito Tejo and and Circuito Olisipo—ask at the tourist office. Several companies run trips on the River Tejo (April to

October). For shorter trips, go to the quays on the Praça do Comércio (▷ 26). For two-hour cruises (Mar–Oct) contact Cruzeiros no Tejo (tel 213 478 030/966 298 558; transtejo.pt).

METRO

Lisbon has an efficient four-line Metropolitano (tel 213 500 115; metrolisboa.pt) that runs from 6.30am to 1am. Buy tickets from booths or at machines at the entrance to stations (*estação*). Tickets cost €1.45 for a single journey in all zones, or you can save money by loading your card with €5, €10 or €15. You can also buy a one-day pass for all zones for €6.15. Validate the pass on your first journey.

STUDENTS AND SENIOR CITIZENS

Certain museums give discounts to students and senior citizens. Discounted coach and rail travel are available on production of an under-26 youth card.

TAXIS

Lisbon's cream- or black-and-green taxis are cheap and can be hailed on the street (a green light means a cab is free) or picked up from ranks such as those at the Baixa-Chiado metro station or Largo do Camões. Taxi stands are on the Rossio, Praça da Figueira and elsewhere; or phone 218 119 000 (Radio Taxis), 217 932 756 (Autocoope) or 218 111 100 (Teletaxis). Fares are 20 percent higher between 9pm and 6am, at weekends and during public holidays.

TRAVEL PASSES

● Buy a rechargeable Viva Viagem card (€0.50), which can be loaded with up to €15. Using this, single bus or metro journeys cost €1.25. A one-day pass (*Bilhete 1 dia*) costs €6.
● *Bilhete de Bordo*: single-journey tickets (€1.45) available on board and only valid in one zone for buses, trams and elevators.
● Lisboa Card: €19 (1 day), €32 (2 day), €40 (3 day) gives free unlimited travel and free entry to most museums and monuments.

FERRIES

Ferries across the Tejo leave from various points throughout the day. Cais do Sodré river station links Lisbon with Cacilhas. There's also a service from Parque das Nações to Cacilhas, and from Belém to Trafaria. Buy tickets at the ferry point; a single costs between €1.20 and €2.75.

VISITORS WITH DISABILITIES

Lisbon's busy, often steep streets can be difficult for visitors with disabilities. Most public buildings and some museums have ramps and other special access. The latest edition of The Accessible Tourism Guide can be obtained from the Secretariado Nacional de Reabilitação ⊠ Avenida Conde Valbom 63 ☎ 215 952 770

WALKING

The best way to discover Lisbon is on foot. Lisbon Walker operates daily and offers a range of guided city tours. Contact them at their Praça do Comércio meeting point or check the website for details.
⊠ Rua do Jardim do Tabaco 126, Sobreloja (office) ☎ 218 861 840; lisbonwalker.com

NEED TO KNOW GETTING AROUND

Essential Facts

ETIQUETTE

Do not wear shorts, miniskirts or skimpy tops in churches, and do not intrude during services. Do not eat or drink in churches. Many churches forbid the use of camera flash and some ban photography. Always be respectful, especially toward people in authority. Smoking is banned in public areas, including public transport.

MONEY

The euro (€) is the official currency of Portugal. Notes come in denominations of 5, 10, 20, 50, 100, 200 and 500 euros, and coins in denominations of 1, 2, 5, 10, 20 and 50 cents, and 1 and 2 euros.

ELECTRICITY
● Current is 220 volts AC (50 cycles), but is suitable for 240 volt appliances. Plugs are of the two-round-pin variety.

EMBASSIES
● Canada: Avenida da Liberdade 198–200, 3rd floor tel 213 164 600, open Mon–Thu 8.30–12.30, 1–5.15, Fri 8.30–1
● United Kingdom: Rua de São Bernardo 33 tel 213 924 000, open Mon–Fri 9–1, 2.30–5.30
● United States: Avenida das Forças Armadas, tel 217 273 300, open Mon–Fri 8–5.

MEDICAL AND DENTAL TREATMENT
● Ask your hotel for details of local doctors who speak English.
● British Hospital (two buildings): Most staff speak English, but there is no emergency department. Torres de Lisboa 217 213 410, Saldanha 213 110 500.
● For emergencies, head to CUF Descobertas, Parque das Nações, tel 210 025 200 (insurance needed).
● Pharmacies' 24-hour rotas are posted on pharmacy doors and in local newspapers. Normal opening times are Mon–Fri 9–1, 3–7, Sat 9–1.

MONEY MATTERS
● Foreign exchange bureaux (*cambios*) and banks with exchange facilities are generally open Mon–Fri 8.30–3. You can also change money at the airport and Santa Apolónia railway station (24-hour services), the main post office and automatic exchange machines.
● Automatic Teller Machines (ATMs), or Multibanco, give credit card cash advances.
● Commission rates on traveler's checks are often high.
● Savings banks or building societies (*caixas*) may charge cheaper rates.
● Credit cards are widely accepted, though some bars and shops do not take cards

OPENING TIMES

● Shops: Traditional shops open Mon–Fri 10–1, 3–7; Sat 10–1. Chain stores open Mon–Sat 10–7. Malls open daily 10–midnight.

● Museums normally open10–1, 2–6. Important museums may remain open all day but times vary. Most are closed on Monday.

● Churches open10–6. Some open only for early morning and evening services.

PUBLIC HOLIDAYS

● 1 Jan: New Year's Day; Feb/Mar: Shrove Tuesday; Good Friday/Easter Monday; 25 Apr: Liberation Day; 1 May: May Day; Corpus Christi (late May or early Jun); 10 Jun: Camões Day; 13 Jun: St. Antony's Day; 15 Aug: Assumption; 5 Oct: Republic Day; 1 Nov: All Saints' Day; 1 Dec: Independence Day; 8 Dec: Immaculate Conception; 25 Dec: Christmas Day.

SENSIBLE PRECAUTIONS

● Don't carry large amounts of cash; use credit cards or traveler's checks.

● Be on your guard against pickpockets on crowded buses, in markets and streets, and beware of strap-cutting thieves.

● Avoid the port, railway station, parks and the Alfama after dark.

TELEPHONES

● The Lisbon area code is 21 and must be dialed regardless of where you call from. It is followed by a seven-digit number. Numbers in this guide are given inclusive of this area code.

● Telecom pay phones are found in bars, cafés, tourist offices, newsagents and street corners.

● Public phones accept euro coins, and increasingly accept credit cards or phone cards, which are available from post offices, kiosks and shops displaying the PT (Portugal Telecom) logo.

● For English-speaking operator for reverse-charge (collect) calls abroad or dialing problems, tel 171 (Europe and intercontinental). Information on international calls, tel 179. National Directory, tel 118.

POSTAL SERVICES

● Post offices are *correios*. Letter boxes are red.

● Lisbon's main post office (*Correio Geral*) is at Praça dos Restauradores 58 ☎ 213 261 370 🕐 Mon–Fri 8.30-6.30.

● There is another large office on Avenida da Liberdade, Rua de Santa Maria 55 ☎ 213 300 811 🕐 Mon–Fri 8am–10pm, Sat, Sun 9–6

● Other post offices usually open Mon–Fri 8 or 9–6. Smaller offices may open 8 or 9–12.30 and 2.30–6. Main offices may open on Saturday morning.

● Buy stamps (*selos*) at post offices or shops displaying the sign CTT Selos or Correio de Portugal Selos.

● Current prices for postcards and letters are €0.90 (EU) and €1.20 (other foreign destinations).

● Airmail is *por avião*. The quickest express service is *Correio Azul*.

EMERGENCIES

Police, Fire or Ambulance ☎ 112

For general enquiries and to report a crime or theft, the Tourist Police have an office open 24 hours a day: ✉ Palácio Foz, Praça dos Restauradores ☎ 213 421 623

Language

Portuguese is a Romance language, so a knowledge of French, Spanish or Italian will help you decipher the written word. The spoken word is a different thing. The pronunciation is difficult, at least at the outset.

USEFUL WORDS AND PHRASES

yes/no	*sim/não*
please	*por favor*
thank you	*obrigado*
	(said by a man)
	obrigada
	(said by a woman)
hello	*olá*
goodbye	*adeus*
good morning	*bom dia*
good afternoon	*boa tarde*
goodnight	*boa noite*
excuse me	*com licença*
I'm sorry	*desculpe*
how much?	*quanto?*
where	*onde*
big/little	*grande/pequeno*
inexpensive	*barato*
expensive	*caro*
today	*hoje*
tomorrow	*amanhã*
yesterday	*ontem*
open/closed	*aberto/fechado*
men	*homens*
women	*senhoras*
I don't understand	*não comprendo*
how much is it?	*quanto custa?*
at what time…?	*a que horas…?*
please help me	*ajude-me por favor*
do you speak English?	*fala inglês?*
How are you?	*Como está?*
Fine, thank you	*Bem obrigado/a*
My name is…	*chamo-me…*
pardon	*desculpe/perdão*

RESTAURANTS

alcohol	*alcool*
beer	*cerveja*
bill	*conta*
bread	*pão*
café	*café*
coffee	*café*
dinner	*jantar*
lunch	*almoço*
menu	*menú/ ementa*
milk	*leite*
pepper	*pimenta*
salt	*sal*
table	*mesa*
tea	*chá*
waiter	*empregado/a*

TOURING

airport	*aeroporto*
boat	*barco*
bus station	*estação de camionetas*
coach	*autocarro*
car	*automóvel*
square	*praça*
street	*rua*
taxi rank	*praça de táxis*
train station	*comboioestação*

EMERGENCY

help	*socorro*
stop	*pare*
stop that thief	*apanhe o ladrão*
police	*polícia*
fire	*fogo*
leave me alone	*deixe-me em paz*
I've lost my purse/wallet	*Perdi o meu porta moedas/a minha-carteira*
Could you call a doctor quickly?	*podia chamar um médico depressa?*
hospital	*hospital*

NUMBERS

0	*zero*
1	*um*
2	*dois*
3	*três*
4	*quatro*
5	*cinco*
6	*seis*
7	*sete*
8	*oito*
9	*nove*
10	*dez*
11	*onze*
12	*doze*
13	*treze*
14	*catorze*
15	*quinze*
16	*dezasseis*
17	*dezassete*
18	*dezoito*
19	*dezanove*
20	*vinte*
100	*cem*
500	*quinhentos*

ACCOMMODATION

does that include breakfast?	*Está incluido o pequeno almoço?*
balcony	*varanda*
air-conditioning	*ar condicionado*
bathroom	*casa de banho*
chambermaid	*camareira*
hot water	*água quente*
key	*chave*
elevator	*elevador*
room	*quarto*
room service	*serviço de quarto*
shower	*duche*
telephone	*telefone*
towel	*toalha*
water	*água*

DAYS OF THE WEEK

Sunday
Domingo

Monday
Segunda-feira

Tuesday
Terça-feira

Wednesday
Quarta-feira

Thursday
Quinta-feira

Friday
Sexta-feira

Saturday
Sábado

NEED TO KNOW LANGUAGE

Timeline

EARTHQUAKE

The Great Earthquake of 1755 began at 9.30am on 1 November—All Saints Day—when many people were at church. The effects of three tremors in 10 minutes were made far worse by a tsunami 6m (19ft) high, and by fires as countless church candles were thrown over. Shock waves were felt as far away as Scotland and Jamaica. An estimated 90,000 people were killed in Lisbon. Corpses were sunk out at sea to halt epidemics. Taxes were suspended and prices fixed by emergency decree. Around 18,000 buildings were destroyed, but the Marquês de Pombal masterminded the reconstruction of the city.

A statue of Afonso Henriques, the first king of Portugal (below left); mosaic on the Arco de Repouso in Faro (below middle); ruins of Lisbon's cathedral after the earthquake of 1755 (below right)

711 The Moors take control of much of Portugal, including Lisbon.

1139 Afonso Henriques, son of a French count and Castilian princess, declares himself first king of "Portucale".

1147 Afonso captures Lisbon from the Moors with soldiers bound for the Second Crusade.

1249 The loss of Faro marks the end of Moorish power in Portugal.

1255 King Afonso III makes Lisbon capital of Portugal, in place of Coimbra.

1385 The Portuguese victory against Castile at the Battle of Aljubarrota secures Portuguese independence for some 200 years.

1580 A crisis in the Portuguese succession allows Philip II of Spain to invade.

1640 The Spanish are overthrown and replaced by the Bragança dynasty of Portuguese kings.

1755 The Great Earthquake destroys two-thirds of Lisbon (▷ panel).

1807 Portugal refuses to join Napoleon's naval blockade of Britain, its ally, and is attacked by a French army.

1810 During ensuing Peninsular Wars, the

Duke of Wellington builds fortifications known as the Lines of Torres Vedras to protect Lisbon.

1834 The end of the "War of the Two Brothers" between Dom Pedro IV, emperor of Brazil, and Dom Miguel.

1908 King Carlos I is assassinated.

1910 The Portuguese monarchy is overthrown and replaced by a republic.

1932 Dr. António de Oliveira Salazar is made Prime Minister and rules as a dictator until 1968.

1974 The Carnation Revolution of 25 April ends some 40 years of dictatorship.

1986 Portugal joins the European Community (now the European Union).

2002 Euro notes and coins come into circulation, replacing the escudo.

2004 Portugal hosts football's Euro 2004.

2008 Pan-European financial crisis effects major infrastructure development in Lisbon.

2014 Lisbon hosts the UEFA Champions League Final.

2017 Economy shows strong signs of revival once minority parties were able to influence Socialist administration.

SEEKING NEW LANDS

In 1419 Henry the Navigator's first square-rigged *barcas* set out in search of a sea route to the Orient. The ship reached Madeira and, eight years later, the Azores. In 1498 four ships under Vasco da Gama left Lisbon and pioneered a sea route to the East Indies, thus breaking the monopoly of Venetian and Ottoman traders in the East. Two years later, in 1500, Pedro Álvares Cabral "discovered" Brazil, whose riches helped to make Portugal the wealthiest country in Europe.

Exhibits in the Museu Militar bear witness to the battles fought in Portugal's turbulent past (below left); Philip II of Spain (below middle); Torre de Belém was built as a lookout post between 1515 and 1520 (below right)

Index

Lisbon 25 Best

WRITTEN BY Tim Jepson, Jackie Staddon and Hilary Weston
UPDATED BY Sally Roy
SERIES EDITOR Clare Ashton
COVER DESIGN Jessica Gonzalez
DESIGN WORK Liz Baldin
COLOR REPROGRAPHICS Ian Little

Published in the United Kingdom by AA Publishing.

ISBN 978-1-6409-7218-6

EIGHTH EDITION

Printed and bound in China by 1010 Printing Group Limited

10 9 8 7 6 5 4 3 2 1

A05671
Maps in this title produced from mapping © MAIRDUMONT / Falk Verlag 2013 and data from openstreetmap.org © OpenStreetMap contributors
Transport map © Communicarta Ltd, UK

We would like to thank the following photographers, companies and picture libraries for their assistance in the preparation of this book.

2-18t AA; 4cl AA/A Kouprianoff; 5c AA/A Mockford & N Bonetti; 6cl AA/T Harris; 6cc AA/T Harris; 6cr AA/P Wilson; 6bl AA/A Kouprianoff; 6cc AA/T Harris; 6cr AA/A Kouprianoff; 7cl AA/A Kouprianoff; 7cc AA/T Harris; 7cr AA/A Mockford & N Bonetti; 7bl AA/T Harris; 7bc AA/T Harris; 7br AA/P Wilson; 10/11t AA/M Birkitt; 10cr AA/A Mockford & N Bonetti; 10/11c AA/T Harris; 10/11b AA/A Mockford & N Bonetti; 11cl AA/A Mockford & N Bonetti; 12b AA/A Mockford & N Bonetti; 13ctl AA/A Mockford & N Bonetti; 13cl AA/A Mockford & N Bonetti; 13bl AA/A Mockford & N Bonetti; 14tcr AA/A Kouprianoff; 14cr AA/A Kouprianoff; 14bcr AA/A Kouprianoff; 14br AA/T Harris; 15b AA/A Mockford & N Bonetti; 16 (i) Visitlisboa; 16 (ii) AA/A Mockford & N Bonetti; 16 (iv) AA/A Kouprianoff; 17 (i) AA/A Kouprianoff; 17 (ii) AA/A Kouprianoff; 16/7 (iii) AA/A Mockford & N Bonetti; 17 (iv) AA/T Harris; 18 (i) AA/T Harris; 18(ii) Visitlisboa; 18 (iii) DigitalVision; 18 (iv) AA/T Harris; 20 AA/A Mockford & N Bonetti; 24l AA/A Kouprianoff; 24r AA/A Mockford & N Bonetti; 25l AA/M Wells; 25r AA/M Wells; 26l AA/A Mockford & N Bonetti; 26c AA/A Mockford & N Bonetti; 26r AA/A Mockford & N Bonetti; 27l AA/T Harris; 27c AA/T Harris; 27r AA/T Harris; 28 AA/A Kouprianoff; 28/29 AA/A Mockford & N Bonetti; 29 AA/A Mockford & N Bonetti; 30t AA/T Harris; 30b AA/M Wells; 31t AA/A Kouprianoff; 32-35t AA/A Mockford & N Bonetti; 36t AA/A Mockford & N Bonetti; 36c AA/A Mockford & N Bonetti; 37-38t AA/A Mockford & N Bonetti; 39 AA/A Kouprianoff; 42tl AA/A Kouprianoff; 42tr AA/A Mockford & N Bonetti; 42/43c AA/A Mockford & N Bonetti; 43t AA/A Mockford & N Bonetti; 43cr AA/T Harris; 44tl AA/M Wells; 44tr AA/M Wells; 45l AA/A Mockford & N Bonetti; 45r AA/A Mockford & N Bonetti; 46l AA/A Kouprianoff; 46r AA/M Birkitt; 47l AA/A Kouprianoff; 47r AA/A Kouprianoff; 48l AA/M Wells; 48/49 AA/A Mockford & N Bonetti; 50/51t AA/A Mockford & N Bonetti; 50b AA/A Kouprianoff; 51b AA/A Kouprianoff; 52 AA/M Wells; 53t AA/A Mockford & N Bonetti; 53c AA/A Mockford & N Bonetti; 54 AA/A Mockford & N Bonetti; 55 AA/A Mockford & N Bonetti; 58l AA/A Mockford & N Bonetti; 58r AA/M Birkitt; 59l AA/A Kouprianoff; 59c AA/A Kouprianoff; 59r AA/A Kouprianoff; 60l AA/A Kouprianoff; 60/61 AA/A Kouprianoff; 62tl AA/A Kouprianoff; 62tr AA/A Kouprianoff; 62cr AA/A Kouprianoff; 63t AA/A Kouprianoff; 63cl AA/A Kouprianoff; 63cr AA/A Kouprianoff; 64t AA/A Kouprianoff; 64bl AA/A Kouprianoff; 64br AA/A Kouprianoff; 65t AA/A Kouprianoff; 66t AA/A Kouprianoff; 67t AA/A Mockford & N Bonetti; 68t-72t AA/P Wilson; 73 AA/A Kouprianoff; 76tl Fundacao Calouste Gulbenkian; 76tr Fundacao Calouste Gulbenkian; 76cr Fundacao Calouste Gulbenkian; 77t Fundacao Calouste Gulbenkian; 77cl Fundacao Calouste Gulbenkian; 77cr Fundacao Calouste Gulbenkian; 78 AA/A Kouprianoff; 79t AA/A Kouprianoff; 79cl AA/A Kouprianoff; 78cr AA/A Kouprianoff; 80l AA/A Kouprianoff; 80r Fundacao Calouste Gulbenkian; 81t AA/P Wilson; 81b AA/M Wells; 82 AA/M Wells; 83 AA/A Kouprianoff; 86l AA/A Kouprianoff; 86/87t AA/A Kouprianoff; 86/87c Visitlisboa; 87r Visitlisboa; 88-89 David Rato/Museu Coleção Berardo; 90l AA/A Kouprianoff; 90r Visitlisboa; 91l AA/A Kouprianoff; 91r AA/A Kouprianoff; 92 AA/A Kouprianoff; 92/93 AA/A Kouprianoff; 93t Visitlisboa; 93c AA/P Wilson; 94t AA/A Kouprianoff; 94b Planetario Calouste Gulbenkian; 95 AA/M Wells; 96 AA/A Mockford & N Bonetti; 97 AA/A Mockford & N Bonetti; 100 AA/A Kouprianoff; 101 AA/A Kouprianoff; 102l AA/M Wells; 102t AA/T Harris; 102b AA/A Mockford & N Bonetti; 103 AA/M Wells; 104-105t AA/T Harris; 104b AA/M Wells; 105bl AA/M Wells; 105br AA/M Wells; 106 AA/T Harris; 108-112t AA/C Sawyer; 108tcr AA/C Sawyer; 108cr AA/D Henley; 108bcr AA/A Mockford & N Bonetti; 108br AA/J Smith; 1114-125t AA/A Mockford & N Bonetti; 122 AA/T Harris; 124bl AA/A Kouprianoff; 124bc AA/C Jones; 124br AA; 125bl AA/A Kouprianoff; 125cb AA; 125br AA/P Wilson

Every effort has been made to trace the copyright holders, and we apologize in advance for any accidental errors. We would be happy to apply the corrections in the following edition of this publication.

Titles in the Series